YOUR POWER WITHIN
INNER GUIDANCE

YOUR POWER WITHIN INNER GUIDANCE

Blanca De La Rosa

First edition: September 2024
© Copyright of the work: Blanca De La Rosa
© Copyright of the edition: Angels Fortune Editions

ISBN: 978-1-83556-265-9 PAPERBACK
ISBN: 978-1-83556-266-6 EBOOK
ISBN: 978-1-83556-267-3 HARDBACK
Correction: Blanca De La Rosa Cover Design: Celia Valero Layout: Celia Valero
Editing by Ma Isabel Montes Ramírez
© Angels Fortune Editions www.angelsfortuneditions.com
All rights reserved for all countries The total or partial reproduction of this book, or the compilation in a computer system, or the transmission in any form or by any means, whether electronic, mechanical or by photocopy, by registration or by other means, neither the loan, rent or any other form of cession of the use of the copy without prior written permission of the copyright owners. «Any form of reproduction, distribution, public communication or transformation of this work can only be carried out with the authorization of its owners, except as otherwise provided by law»
Formatted by HMDPUBLISHING

LEARN TO MAKE LEMONADE
The Optimist

*Author: Clarence Edwin Flynn
(November 1940), The Rotarian*

> "Life handed him a lemon,
> As Life sometimes will do.
> His friends looked on in pity,
> Assuming he was through.
> They came upon him later,
> Reclining in the shade
> In calm contentment, drinking
> A glass of lemonade."

"Choose to be optimistic, it feels better."
— The Dalai Lama

CONTENTS

PROLOGUE: Meaning of Title and Cover Design 9

01. My Chosen Path 11
    The End of My Life as I knew It. 12
    Opposites Attract.. 18
    What's in a Name—Reclaiming My Identify 20
    Spiritual Awakening. 23
    The Reunion 26

02. The Soul's Journey 29
    What is a Soul journey?.. 30
    Your Inner Guidance—Look Within 33
    Discovering Your Life's Purpose—Why Am I Here? 40
    Choose Your Own Path.. 45
    Your Soul's Journey 50

03. Walking the Walk of Your Chosen Path 55
    Self-Acceptance—Embrace Your Uniqueness 57
    Project Confidence—Boost Your Self Esteem.. 61
    Master Your Fears.. 67
    Shake Off the Bitterness. 73
    Find Someone or Something to Lean on 79
    Embrace New Beginnings. 82
    Walking the walk of your chosen path. 85

04. Easing the Walk of Your Chosen Path 87
    Chronic Stress. 88
    Make Sleeping a Priority 90
    Laugh More. 92
    Listen to Music.. 94
    Just Say "No" 96
    Strive for Financial Freedom. 97
    Choose Peace and Happiness 100
    Easing the Walk of Your Chosen Path 102

05. Parenting—To Be or Not To Be. 103
    The Teenage Brain. 106
    Is parenting over-rated?.. 108

06. **What About Religion?** 113
    Spirituality versus Organized Religion. 117
07. **The End of Your Chosen Path.** 119
    Fear of Death 120
    Transformative Voyage for a New Beginning 121
    Departure of the Soul. 123
    Deathbed Companions 125
    Your Legacy and Beyond 130
    Tapestry of Life and Death 131

ABOUT THE AUTHOR 135
BIBLIOGRAPHY 143

PROLOGUE:
MEANING OF TITLE AND COVER DESIGN

The title "*Your Power Within - Inner Guidance*" emphasizes the themes of personal empowerment and wisdom by suggesting that each individual harbors a source of strength and knowledge inside themselves, which is complemented by the notion of inner guidance. It acknowledges that recognizing and tapping into one's own power is the initial step on the path to gaining profound wisdom, with inner guidance serving as an instrumental resource, unlocking their full potential and navigate life's journey with confidence and insight.

The lotus flower is a powerful symbol that complements these themes. In many spiritual traditions, the lotus represents purity, enlightenment, self-regeneration, and rebirth. Its characteristics are a fitting metaphor for personal growth and the quest for wisdom. Despite growing in muddy waters, the lotus blooms immaculately above the surface, which parallels the human ability to rise above challenges and limitations to achieve a state of clarity and enlightenment.

Incorporating the lotus flower into the cover design visually communicates these ideas. It signifies blossoming into one's best self, guided by the inner wisdom that the title speaks of. The unfolding petals represent the layers of personal discovery and the expansion of one's inner power, while the clean, radiant bloom suggests the attainment of spiritual enlightenment and the realization of one's potential.

The lotus flower is a complex symbol that embodies the path to enlightenment, the resilience of the spirit, the significance of detachment, and the splendor of creation, resonating across different spiritual avenues. It holds profound spiritual significance across various cultures and religions. The flower is commonly associated with purity, inner strength and tranquility, but its symbolism extends beyond that. The flower plays a symbolic role in various religions such as Hinduism, Buddhism, Sikhism, and Jainism. Given its deep symbolic meanings and connection to religion, the lotus flower is considered one of the most sacred plants.

The lotus flower's journey from the depths to the light encapsulates the spiritual path of humans, echoing the soul's ascent from the confines of the physical world to the liberation of the spiritual realm. Its beauty and grace serve as a powerful reminder of our own potential to rise above challenges and bloom with resilience and grace.

Furthermore, the lotus embodies the principle of detachment. Each night, it retracts from the water, symbolizing the need to withdraw from worldly desires and materialistic ties. This act serves as a poignant reminder to maintain spiritual purity amidst life's impurities and attachments.

Overall, the title and the imagery of the lotus flower work together to convey a message of hope, transformation, and the infinite possibilities that lie within the realm of personal empowerment and inner wisdom.

CHAPTER 1

MY CHOSEN PATH

My chosen path revolved around family—the compass that guided me, the anchor that steadied my soul. Their laughter echoed through the hallways of our home, weaving threads of support and stability. In their eyes, I glimpsed purpose—a shared journey where we thrived together.

Throughout the years, my husband and I nurtured our love. We weathered storms, danced through seasons, and reveled in the simple joy of being together. Dancing and travel became the rhythm of our lives—a harmonious duet that echoed across continents and our kitchen alike.

As we planned the celebration of our 50th wedding anniversary, excitement bubbled within us. We were about to honor a magnificent tapestry—a labor of love woven with threads of commitment, shared memories, and cherished moments. Our children, grandchildren, and extended family would gather, and amidst laughter and tears, we'd celebrate the legacy we had created—a legacy that transcended time.

The End of My Life as I knew It

August 4, 2023, was the beginning of the end of my life as I knew it. The doctors diagnosed my husband, Danilo Cespedes, with pancreatic cancer and gave him six to eight months to live.

We were both in shock, trying to come to terms with the fact that our lives would never be the same. The days seemed to blur together as we navigated through the whirlwind of doctors' appointments, treatment plans, and emotional turmoil.

As we digested the finality of the diagnosis, Danilo was afraid at the prospect of dying. I was delicately trying to appease him but to no avail.

I often shared with him my views on the afterlife, astral travel, celestial beings, and other mystical subjects. While he would listen, he seemed skeptical of these concepts. However, one morning in 2022, he awoke with a sense of wonder and excitedly said to me, "Blanca, I went to the other side last night. It was so peaceful. I saw my parents and friends and it felt so good to be there. I now understand what you have been telling me about the other side and soul travel. I was there." After sharing this profound experience, we moved on from the topic and never mentioned it again.

Early September 2023 as I was driving to the hospital in tears feeling helpless, not knowing what I could do to help him. I suddenly remembered that conversation from the prior year and knew that I had to remind him.

When I got to the hospital, I said to him, "Do you remember that dream that you told me about where your soul traveled to the other side? How it felt to be there, and that there was nothing to fear about going there. That was to prepare for this experience so that you wouldn't be scared." After we had that conversation, his attitude changed. He was no longer afraid and accepted his fate with courage. During his illness, I continued to share with him my beliefs and told him that after he passed he had to find a way to come back and tell me whether I was right or wrong.

As the months passed, we clung to each other for support, finding solace in the small moments of normalcy amidst the chaos. We tried to make the most of the time we had left together, cherishing every moment, never leaving one another's side.

Despite the overwhelming sadness that consumed us, we found moments of hope and strength in each other. We faced the challenges ahead with courage and resilience, determined to make the most of the time we had left.

As the days turned into weeks and the weeks turned into months, we found joy in the simple things, treasuring every smile, every laugh, every I love you, and every moment of peace we shared in the confinement of our home.

During the final two weeks of his life, Danilo talked about visions of his mother and other deceased loved ones, which provided profound comfort. He seemed to be very comforted by his mother's presence as he spoke with her telling her that he was depending on her to guide him in this journey. The communication with his mother helped Danilo approach the end of his life on earth with a level of acceptance that surprised many of his family members.

Danilo had always said that he wanted to die before me and when the time came, he wanted it to be just the two of us. The day before he passed Hospice had told us he would pass within the next 24 hours. His three sons and one of their wives were in the room. At about 11:00 p.m., I told everyone to go home get a good night's sleep and come back the next day. After they left, I said to him, "Everyone is gone now. It's just the two of us now, just like you wanted. Please let me know when it's time. Don't leave without saying goodbye."

As some cancer patients approach death, breathing patterns can change and secretions may collect in the throat. This creates a rattling sound known as the death rattle. It is a part of the dying process.

While the sound is unpleasant, the person emitting the death rattle usually feels no pain or discomfort. The death rattle signals that death is near. On average, a person usually lives for approximately 24 hours after the death rattle and the dying process begins.

I lay down by his side, holding his hand. Despite the loud sound of the death rattle, I dozed off. I don't know for sure what alerted me. I thought I detected a difference in the rattle and awakened at about 6:15 a.m. Somehow, he found a way to make sure I was awake and present when he took his last breath.

On January 29, 2024, at 6:35 a.m. my lifelong partner and best friend of 52 years departed from this world, creating an irreplaceable void in my heart. The profound sorrow I was feeling rendered my heart speechless, unable to express itself. The echoes of my husband's existence remain in my soul, reverberating in my chest every time I think of him.

Amid my grief, I found solace in the love we shared and the memories we created together. And though my life had taken an unexpected turn, I knew I would always carry his spirit with me, guiding me through the darkness and reminding me of the strength we had found in each other.

I am grateful for the years filled with heartfelt and unwavering love, along with the deep respect we held for each other. Together, we shed tears and reveled in the happiness and laughter that define a lifetime. Disagreements between us were infrequent, and when they occurred, they were petty quarrels over insignificant issues that quickly faded away, leaving behind no resentment or silent treatment. I will always cherish the memories of the little things and precious moments that made up our 52-year journey together.

When Danilo passed away, I felt disoriented. I had spent eight months nursing him and sitting by his bedside as he battled pancreatic cancer, disengaging from all other activities. After his death and dealing with final arrangements, I felt like a blank page with no direction, unsure of what I should be doing. I had no clue what the future had in store for me without my lifelong partner and best friend by my side.

His death marked a significant turning point, the final chapter of my life on earth with Danilo. Yet, I was confident that our bond would persist in a spiritual form. The bonds we share with our loved ones does not end with their death; they simply transform. Maintaining a positive connection beyond death is vital for the well-being of souls on both sides of the curtain of life on earth and the other side. I conveyed this belief, which brought great solace to Danilo in his final days. He would often tell me, "I will always be by your side and will be waiting for you on the other side, but you better not show up with another guy."

Since his passing, I've had two significant spiritual experiences with my beloved husband.

In mid-March, my sister called me in an emotional state. She cried as she said, "Blanca, I went for a reading with Denise at Celestial Circle and Danilo came through. He was very chatty, talking about the events of his memorial service and in awe of the number of people that had attended. He wants to talk with you and asked that you call."

You may think, where does one call to the other side, 1800-HEAVEN? Of course, I knew she meant to make an appointment with Denise at Celestial Circle, and I did. My appointment was a couple of days later that week. When I connected with the medium, she said, "There is someone here that wants to say something."

I said "Okay" in apprehension, not sure what was going to be said. To my shock and pleasant surprise, she said, "He said tell her she was right."

I immediately burst into tears, knowing that it was my dearly departed husband coming back as I had asked him to find a way to come back and tell me 'right' or 'wrong'. During the forty-minute reading, he told me how grateful he was for the care I had given him during his illness and that he could not have asked for a better nurse. He also said that if I had not agreed to marry him, he would've never married as his life plan included one wife and that was me but only if I agreed to marry him. He said that he would always be by my side and that of our family. He asked that I not give up on writing as he would inspire me through my journey as an author. Although I cried for days after this experience, it was extremely comforting for me to know I could maintain communication with my husband. That our relationship would continue on a spiritual level as he would still be my most ardent supporter.

The second experience was a much more tangible and supernatural one. In mid-June, as I slept on my side, I felt my bed move and sensed some commotion behind me. I tried to turn around to see what was going on behind me and what had caused the bed to move, but I was immobilized. I was conscious but could not move my body. Just then, my soul exited my body, and I saw Danilo lying down beside me. He was looking strong, vibrant, and handsome, appearing to be in his late 40s. I was so happy to see him. I touched him, and he felt real.

I said, "Oh my God, you came back, it's really you," I babbled on. He responded, "I only have ten minutes, then I have to go." During those ten minutes, he told me that he was happy on the other side and thanked me for our shared experience and for taking such good care of him during his illness. However, he was concerned as he could see how his illness was taking a toll on me. Every day, he would pray it would be his last so that he could release me from the burden. He said, "You look much better now." I told him that taking care of him was my pleasure and I would not have wanted it any other way because I knew that if it were me on that bed, he would've never left my side nor allowed anyone else to care for me. He assured me that he would always be by my side and would always love me. This experience was very comforting for me, knowing that he was doing well and that we could still communicate.

My partner's absence left me grappling with a mix of emotions - grief, confusion, and a sense of loss. I felt adrift and unsure of how to move forward without him by my side as his absence upended my life, causing the routine and familiarity of my life to disappear. I felt like a part of me was missing, and I struggled to envision a future without him. For example, we shared a deep connection through our travels to many different countries and the mere thought of boarding an airplane without him evoked powerful emotions.

There was no place I wanted to go and confined myself to our bedroom in an intentional search for solitude. I reduced my life to the simple things: reading, writing, watching Lifetime movies, and sleeping a lot. I'd spend days in my bedroom, as it was my sanctuary where I had spent quality time with him. Being in that room comforted me, as his presence was still palpable. I only ventured out of my bedroom to the kitchen to get something to eat.

Although I looked forward to talking to friends and family from time to time, I avoided meeting anyone, because I wanted to be alone in that kind of hermetic bubble I had created solely and exclusively for myself and my spiritual connection with Danilo. I did not want to know what was going on outside of my little bubble whether it was someone else's personal drama or national drama on the news. Intentionally isolating myself, creating a cocoon of solitude where the outside world would only intrude when I gave it permission to do so. I recognized that even as I secluded myself in my own isolated world, life continued to unfold. The world spins, seasons change, and stories unfold. As I was in hibernation, winter gave way to spring, and spring blossomed into summer, yet I stayed within my cocoon. Nevertheless, I recognized the need to reconnect gradually with the rest of the world. Peeking from the confines of my cocoon, I began to explore the world that had continued to evolve outside my secluded haven.

As I navigated the practicalities of life without him, I also had to come to terms with the emotional void his absence had left behind. Memories of our time together flooded my mind, both comforting and painful in their reminder of what I had lost.

Amid this uncertainty, I recognized that it was essential to reinvent myself and my existence in his absence. It became imperative for me to discover the new direction my journey should take now that I was on my own. It was a daunting task, but I knew I had to move forward, to honor his memory while also carrying on my own with my destiny for part two of my life. It was going to be a journey of self-discovery and healing, one that would ultimately lead me to a place of acceptance and peace.

Opposites Attract

Danilo and I were like night and day, yet as the saying goes, "opposites attract." Despite our stark differences, we shared a 52-year relationship filled with its ups and downs—thankfully, with the ups far outweighing the downs.

Reflecting on my life with Danilo, I thought a lot about why opposites attract and concluded that the reason opposites attract is to bring balance into one another's lives. Balance is critical for leading a fulfilling and happy life, as having too much of anything is not good for you.

Our 52 year relationship taught me you are not someone else's other half or better half. In order to have a long-lasting relationship, you must acknowledge your individuality before you can pronounce yourself a couple. Know yourself, your wants and needs.

Danilo was an inevitable part of my life's journey, despite my initial reluctance. His determination was unwavering as he continued to court me for several years until I finally agreed to go out with him. His refusal to accept rejection and his repeated efforts to win me over suggested that he, being a few years older, knew deep down inside that this relationship was part of our combined destiny.

The cosmic connection center of the universe had ensured our relationship would happen. Or, at least, that we would meet.

- Danilo worked in the produce section of the supermarket where my family shopped. I first noticed him when I was about thirteen years old, while at the supermarket with my mother. He was always trying to get my attention, and I hated it. I tried to avoid that section of the supermarket. You may think that thirteen is too young, but I was a mature-looking and acting thirteen-year-old.

- He was the best friend and schoolmate of the boyfriend of one of my first cousins. He once sent a message to me through my cousin, saying, "Tell her that if I don't marry her, I will never marry." My reply had been, "He should prepare for a life of bachelorhood."

- He was friends with my father from the local barbershop and from fixing cars in the parking lot of the building where I lived, although Danilo did not know that his friend was my father.
- His sister was my mother's hairdresser. He lived with his sister, half a city block from our apartment building.

The synchronistic events that culminated in our meeting could not have been coincidental—it was our destiny—our life's journey; that brought us together to experience this destined relationship.

We had three sons, five grandchildren, and one great granddaughter. Danilo was a great dad and Papa. As we raised our children, Danilo was ahead of his time as a "Mr. Mom." In the early to mid-eighties, this role wasn't common, especially in our machismo laden Latino community where childcare was often considered a woman's responsibility. Fortunately, Danilo stepped up and shared household duties, taking care of the family. We found the perfect balance, capitalizing on each other's strengths. Despite challenges, we persevered, emphasizing that household tasks shouldn't disproportionately fall on women.

Unbeknownst to him, Danilo was a role model by example. In the last six months of his life, numerous young men called to express their gratitude for his being an exemplary model of a father and husband for them to emulate. These were the same children that visited our home throughout the years.

With Danilo's unwavering support, I achieved my educational pursuits, a successful career with ExxonMobil, and my post- retirement career as an author. He was not only supportive but accommodating even when I was being somewhat unreasonable.

What's in a Name—Reclaiming My Identify

Do you ever feel you need a reprieve from your day-to-day life? You want to unplug from your daily routine so you can rejuvenate.

For forty-plus years, I had followed an orderly, goody-two-shoes kind of life, always doing the right thing, and following the rules. There were no crazy stories, no unhealthy, lustful relationships. No secrets. No intrigue. I'm sure many would say, "What a boring life." That could be in the eyes of some. But it had been a busy and productive life thus far.

There's a common saying that one's true life begins after 40. The notion that life begins at 40 is a popular adage, with a wealth of life experiences contributing to this notion. It suggests that people often reach a stage of self-realization and confidence at this age. While it's not universally true for everyone, many do find that the accumulation of life experiences by the time they reach 40 provides a clearer understanding of their personal desires and values.

For some, maturity marks a period of gaining self-confidence because not everyone has lived their life the way they wanted. For example, some people didn't know themselves or their true desires, so they followed others advice instead. Or they might have chosen or been compelled into a relationship with the wrong life partner. A fear of social judgement often leads them to take the path of least resistance.

Sometimes with age and the realization that half of one's life has passed comes the liberation from old fears and complexes. For such individuals, turning 40 is a sort of blossoming a period of growth and empowerment, where individuals feel liberated from past constraints and are more inclined to focus on personal fulfillment and new beginnings. Once the kids are grown, there's more opportunity to focus on self-discovery, to sever ties with the past, and to forge ahead with new relationships. It's a period of renewal and self-empowerment that many embrace.

However, it's important to recognize that personal growth and the pursuit of self-confidence can happen at any age, and life's journey is unique for each individual. Some may find this blossoming earlier or later than 40, and that's perfectly okay. Everyone's timeline is different, and each person's story unfolds in its own way. The key is to remain open to growth and change, regardless of age.

From 1975 to 1998, everything had been about school, work, raising children, maintaining a relationship, and keeping a home. I transitioned from being a daughter to being a wife, mother, student, and employee. There hadn't been a time when I focused on me—on what I wanted to do. The idea of blossoming at this age definitely resonated for me as I had spent many years prioritizing the needs of others. With these responsibilities lessening, I found myself free to pursue my own interests and passions.

I was exhausted, and I wanted to take and make the time to focus on my wants and needs. I needed to nourish and energize my soul. But here's the thing: I had been taking care of so many people for so long that I did not know where or how to take care of "me." That "me" that I had sacrificed to marriage, motherhood, and work. That "me" that I hadn't had the chance to get to know since I married at 18 years of age.

I needed to get to know myself as an adult. Throughout the years, I hadn't stopped long enough to get acquainted with the adult "me." I intimately acquainted myself with Blanca Céspedes, the wife, mother, and employee. I did not know Blanca De La Rosa, the adult.

Some may argue it's just a name, no big deal. Right? Some may even say that I'm overreacting and exaggerating the symbolic power of my name. But everyone recognizes themselves by their name, which represents their personal history.

The Céspedes name represented my husband's history and heritage; it was his identity, his life, not mine. I wanted to explore the powerful influence my birth name would wield over my life—the life I'd been born to live.

The first thing I had to do on the road to that reprieve was to ease the burden that changing my name had imposed. I had to reclaim my identity. I spent twenty-three years living as someone I could not fully embrace.

Over time, using my married name became bothersome. I resorted to introducing myself by my first name only. A coworker would tease me, saying, "What are you, like Pele or Madonna, known by your first name only?"

A name change after marriage is a personal decision that women make for several reasons. I, like so many other women, took it as a given, as it was the tradition. Some husbands take it personally if their wives do not adopt their married names, claiming: one family, one name. However, no one should feel guilty or pressured either way.

For me, it was not the right decision. Even after twenty-three years of being a Céspedes, which was five years longer than I had been a De La Rosa, I still could not get accustomed to using someone else's name. In 1998, I reverted to using my birth name. Ahh, what a relief.

It was a liberating sensation akin to the relief one experiences when taking off a tight garment or shoes. This marked the beginning of my journey of self-discovery to acquaint myself with my adult self. The name change had empowered and invigorated me with a newfound sense of strength and vitality. I was born a De La Rosa, and I intend to die a De La Rosa.

The paperwork required to change my name legally was tedious, but the hardest part of the entire process was the discussion I had with my husband. It was tough, as he immediately took it personally. It was difficult for him to comprehend my sense of losing my identity, feeling disconnected from my roots, and the unnaturalness I felt in using his name. He was not happy, and it took him a while to acclimate to the name change. He eventually relented, accepting the name change with one caveat: he did not want anyone to call him Mr. De La Rosa.

Two years after the name change, I took the finding myself a step further and Danilo and I divorced, but we remained friends, best friends, supporting each other's endeavors. Our friendship was solid and dependable providing a foundation of support and understanding that empowered us to face life's challenges with confidence and strength.

Despite the uncertainties about the direction our separation might take us, we proceeded, granting one another the room to grow through the separation and transition.

Spiritual Awakening

In late 1999, my son told me about a woman he had seen on *The Larry King Show* named Sylvia Browne. I thought "how interesting" but took no action to follow-up. A week later, I saw one of her books, *The Other Side and Back*, while shopping. I thought, "Wow, what a coincidence," and purchased the book. I read the book and discovered that she had written about a lot of the philosophies that I had instinctively known and believed but hadn't been able to substantiate or articulate.

I later discovered *The Journey of the Soul Series*. In this series, Sylvia shares her forty years of investigation and research on religious and spiritual issues. I found the research profound, spiritually moving, and eminently logical. I attended events hosted by Sylvia Browne, where she shared her research and experience. During those events, I discovered other events organized by Hay House and their Wisdom Community.

The Hay House events and authors gave me the confidence to embrace my spirituality and come out of the "spiritual closet." Sylvia Browne put me on the path to spiritualism and changed my life most profoundly.

Sylvia Browne was the founder of the Society of Novus Spiritus, a community of Gnostic Christians. *Gnostic* is a Greek word, meaning "seekers of truth and knowledge." The Gnostic philosophy encourages you to think and question everything. It states that you should read it, question it, take what works for you, and leave the rest behind, even if "it" is a philosophy from another religion or region.

There is no condemnation, judgment, or demeaning of your soul. You are not a sinner; everyone is worthy in the eyes of God.

It is about becoming a better person and perfecting your soul. The message is always positive and encouraging. Even though I could not identify or articulate what my instincts had been telling me, the Gnostic philosophy is what I had instinctively known and believed.

Since discovering this philosophy, I am elated about my spirituality. The Gnostic philosophy provided the wind that my sail needed to find its course. I had finally found spirituality without organized religion.

There comes a time for each of us when we must decide the "truth" for ourselves. If what you consider the truth aligns with your religion, hooray! If not, then you must find and align yourself with people and organizations that match your beliefs. Belief is a matter of individual choice and when it coincides with one's religious teachings, it's indeed a moment of joy.

Despite being alone for three years after my divorce, I did not feel lonely. I took comfort and pure joy in discovering my spirituality. There was so much for me to learn and discover. I dedicated most of my free time to attending Hay House events in different cities, reading, researching, and writing. I needed this period of "alone time" to develop my spirituality without the distraction and burden of a relationship. I had enough distractions with my career, business travel schedule, and getting my children on the road to complete independence.

I loved my new life, spirituality, and the person who had emerged. The ironic thing about the metamorphosis was that I retreated from the people who were the closest to me, hence the divorce. Not that they were no longer good enough for me, it was more about my trying to find myself and my place in life and trying to determine how those people fit into my life.

Following the Gnostic philosophy had been rewarding and self- gratifying. I wish I had learned about it earlier in my life. It would have influenced my response in critical situations. But then, my life was so busy with family, school, business travel, and career that I had not had the time to stop and think about anything else. In life, everything happens when it is supposed to. Not a minute earlier.

I embarked on a journey of personal growth, transformation, and exploration. The profound experience allowed me to perceive my life and the lives of those around me in a new light—an insight I wouldn't have gained with a less enlightened consciousness. My spiritual foundation wouldn't have been possible without the insights I gained from reading Hay House books and taking part in Wisdom Community events.

This shift in consciousness was part of my maturation as a spiritual being; it was part of my personal growth as Blanca De La Rosa. My professional, educational, and personal accomplishments paled compared to the spiritual awakening, enlightenment, shift in consciousness, and inner peace that finding myself gave me.

The Reunion

After three years, Danilo and I had finally moved on to the final stage of the separation, where we were truly living independent lives but remaining best friends. We were no longer codependent. We had undone the tightly twined bonds of the previous thirty years.

But here's the thing: that separate lives thing did not last long. After the holidays in 2003, four full years after the divorce and finding myself, Danilo and I started dating. In April 2003, we made our relationship official and let family and friends know we would be remarrying. We remarried on June 28, 2003, in a chapel in Las Vegas. There were no guests, no family, just the two of us. It was the most romantic time of our lives. And we lived happily thereafter.

What the hay? What was the purpose of the last four years? The separation, the divorce, and the drama?

The separation was a journey to rediscover my identity, my individuality and connecting with my inner self and spiritual path. It had little to do with my relationship with Danilo and was more about stepping away from the hustle and bustle of my daily routine and looking within to find enlightenment.

During the time of our separation, I had changed my name, gone on a four-year sabbatical, and emerged as the person I am today. During those four years of metamorphosis, there had been a lot of turmoil in both my professional and personal lives, as I was transforming into the new "me." I got to know and understand Blanca De La Rosa. Okay, so I'm a slow learner. But I learned a valuable lesson. I learned that you must be an individual before you can couple with someone else. You must know and understand your soul before you can commit to a soul mate. *"Spiritual awakening is not about changing who you are, but letting go of who you are not."—Deepak Chopra*

Life's journey is a winding path, full of twists and turns. As I step forward into the second part of my life without the support of my lifelong partner, I must consider the choices that will continue to lead me toward growth, fulfillment, and purpose. Whether I embark on a new career, my passion for writing, or discover a new personal quest, I wholeheartedly embrace the journey with curiosity and courage.

I started writing this book hoping it would help me identify my purpose after the passing of my partner of 52 years. Now, as I navigate this new chapter in my life without my best friend by my side, I seek guidance and clarity. Through my writing and research, I learned I had to be patient with myself and the process proceeding gradually, embracing each day as it presents itself. Digging my purpose from the depth of my subconsciousness was going to require time, work, and patience.

Only time will tell where I am headed but I am excited by the prospects of what the future holds.

CHAPTER 2

THE SOUL'S JOURNEY

*The Soul's journey is not a straight path...it's a cycle.
Life after life we return to evolve...to grow from seeing and
understanding deeper spiritual truths*
- Muses by a Mystic

The essence of the soul's journey lies in accumulating and comprehending experiences. Each action, spoken word, and emotion contributes to this path of learning, growth, and evolution. It's a path of learning, experiencing, and evolving.

What is a Soul journey?

A soul journey is a route of spiritual and personal development that enables us to discover our passions, connect with our inner selves, and align with our greater purpose. It's a journey to realizing our individual potential and reaching our destiny. Throughout our journey, we seek to find purpose and meaning beyond the material world. At that point, the concept of a soul journey becomes a reality. The soul journey is a profound concept that has been embraced across various cultures and spiritual practices throughout history. It speaks to the universal human quest for deeper understanding and purpose. In modern times, as more individuals seek fulfillment beyond material success, the idea of a soul journey has grown in popularity.

This journey is not just a metaphorical path but a transformative process. As we navigate through life, the challenges, obstacles, and opportunities we face are the catalysts for growth, self-discovery, and enlightenment. They compel us to look inward, to question, and to seek truths that lie beyond the surface of our daily existence. Each step taken on this journey contributes to the evolution of the soul, allowing us to become more aligned with our true essence and potential. Every experience, whether perceived as good or bad, is an invitation to learn more about ourselves and the universe we are a part of.

One of the key aspects of the soul journey is discovering our purpose. Our soul incarnated on Earth with a specific purpose—to contribute something unique to our family, community, or the world at large. Noteworthy that the idea of reincarnation and differing lifetimes is a spiritual belief and not scientifically proven. However, it offers a framework for understanding the greater context of our soul's journey across multiple lifetimes. Many believe that souls choose from four main types of lifetimes when they incarnate. Each lifetime serves a purpose, and our soul's journey encompasses a mix of these types.

1. **Contribution Lifetime:** A contribution lifetime involves fulfilling a specific role or purpose within a group, which may include being

a public figure and making significant contributions to society. In these lifetimes, souls aim to make a difference. This may encompass introducing a pivotal invention that revolutionizes the lives of many individuals, supporting a substantial (ethnic, political, religious) community meaningfully, or assuming a leadership position (like Prime Minister). Alternatively, it could involve advocating for a particular cause. These souls incarnate to expand through learning. These lifetimes focus on acquiring knowledge, wisdom, and experiences. They offer opportunities for growth and self-discovery. The soul's aim is to contribute something meaningful and leave a lasting impact.

2. **Service/Support Lifetime:** A Support lifetime is characterized by a soul's incarnation intending to aid another in their journey of learning life's lessons. To illustrate, imagine life as a grand play where each of us has a role to fulfill. To experience certain events, we often rely on the participation of others. For instance, if you have a child with a chronic illness or special needs, they may require extensive support from you throughout their life. This caregiving experience might teach you valuable lessons, such as patience, love, acceptance, or resilience. These souls emphasize helping and guiding others on their paths. Souls choose these lifetimes to assist others in their evolution. They function as guides, mentors, or helpers, supporting fellow souls on their journeys. Support lifetimes emphasize service and compassion. A humanitarian worker who travels to disaster-stricken areas to provide aid and relief to those in need, embodying compassion and selflessness is another example.

3. **Learning Lifetime:** The focus of this lifetime is on acquiring knowledge and wisdom through various experiences. For example, a young artist who is passionate about painting and, throughout their life, encounters challenges and opportunities that shape their artistic journey. They learn different techniques, experiment with styles, and express their emotions through their art. Throughout their lifetime, they encounter various challenges and opportunities that teach them about creativity, perseverance, and the beauty of self-expression. Each painting becomes a lesson in itself, contributing to the artist's growth and understanding of the world around

them. A young entrepreneur who starts a business from scratch, facing many obstacles, and learning valuable lessons about resilience, innovation, and leadership is another example.

4. **Holiday or Balance Lifetime:** Souls sometimes choose a holiday lifetime when they have had a series of intense learning lifetimes and so this time around they want a bit of a rest. In this life, they are choosing to have happy experiences which will resource them for future lifetimes and give them a break on the soul level. Their primary focus is enjoying planet earth.

These are individuals who effortlessly navigate through life, as opportunities are constantly presented to them from all directions. They rarely encounter difficulties effortlessly bringing their desires into reality, more so than the average person. These are joyful, carefree lifetimes where souls simply enjoy existence, savoring life's pleasures and pausing from the usual challenges. During the balance lifetimes, souls rest, play, and recharge. Life has been relatively easy; may be born into a loving, probably financially comfortable family and haven't experienced many or any major challenges in life. An example would be a teacher who imparts knowledge to students while also nurturing their own personal growth through hobbies, family life, and community involvement. A person born with a silver spoon.

Each of these examples illustrates a different path that a soul might choose in its journey through various lifetimes Discovering our soul's purpose can be a lifelong quest, and it often involves exploring our passions, interests, and talents. Your soul's journey is unique to you, and it may take time and patience to fully discover and align with your purpose.

The concept of a soul journey can provide a powerful framework for understanding your life and discovering your purpose. By connecting with your inner self, reflecting on your passions and interests, and following your intuition, you can embark on a transformative journey of personal and spiritual growth.

Your Inner Guidance—Look Within

Fortunately, we are all equipped with an internal compass that will help us navigate our individual paths. For thousands of years, seers and sages have encouraged us to look within for the truth we seek. This internal compass provides all the guidance and tools you need along the journey of your soul. This innate GPS (Global Positioning System) is your inner self, inner spirit, intuition, gut feeling, inner voice, insight, or whatever you want to call it.

Finding answers to our most personal questions can initially be a daunting task. Accessing the depths of our hearts, where our soul lives, may seem like a challenge, but it is straightforward. This inner sanctuary is the key to unlocking our true potential, although it may be the most difficult aspect to reach. Once we arrive there, a world of possibilities opens before us, allowing us to manifest all that we are capable of as human beings.

Whenever you feel overwhelmed, alone, and afraid of one of life's challenges, turn to your inner GPS for guidance. The Path you have chosen in this lifetime may seem long and lonely, but you can turn to the instruction manual inside your soul to guide you. Children aren't born with an instruction manual to guide parents, but they are born with an instruction manual to help them navigate their own lives as they travel their chosen path. You just need to stop, listen, and follow your inner guidance. There is an answer to all your questions inside your soul. You don't have to feel lost and afraid. The fear, sorrow, and anxiety will disappear as you discover the answer within your heart and soul. This will provide you with the resilience required to persevere, as you recognize that 'this too shall pass.'

Your subconscious can visualize and realize an amazing future if you give yourself permission to tap into your inner source. Only you can access what is inside of you, bring it forward, and make it a reality. Your accomplishments and the realization of your dreams are up to you because your true potential far exceeds what you have tapped into thus far.

Life is about free will, options, choices, and what we make of the opportunities presented to us. There are no such things as right or wrong decisions, as each decision will provide experiences and lessons necessary for your development. The lessons learned and experiences gained have shaped not only the person you are today but also the individual you will become in the future.

You need to stop, reflect, and capture the lesson that each experience delivers, so that you can grow and move forward. In life, nothing happens by accident or coincidence, and every experience is merely a stepping-stone on the path you will walk in this lifetime. If you find yourself unable to tap into your inner voice, temporarily disconnect from others. Take a time-out. Go away to reflect and get back in touch with your truth. Give yourself some time and space to get away from the day-to-day noise, schedule, and expectations of others.

Move away from the distractions by doing an activity that requires you to spend time alone with your thoughts. This will mean something different to everyone. For some, it may be physical activity: a long walk, run, jog, gym, Pilates, yoga, or other activity. For others, it may be something quieter, like meditating, praying, or journaling. It could be the first thing you do in the morning or the last thing you do in the evening. Pick an activity, time, and place that works for you.

The point is to move away from anything that distracts you from being alone with your thoughts in an independent and self-sufficient state of mind that enables you to contemplate a life review and potential changes for your future or deal with certain challenges you may be facing. This is your time to rejuvenate and connect with your inner source. It is your time to tap into the wealth of knowledge and wisdom that lives within you.

If you get off course and a certain decision you have made is not aligned with your true essence, your inner voice will second-guess your decisions and motives. We need to satisfy that inner voice that gives us the signal that it needs to reroute to get us back on track to ensure that we accomplish our soul's mission. This is like the GPS device that signals it is rerouting when you do not follow the exact route it has mapped out to reach your destination.

As you go through life and come upon challenging situations, you will seek many external sources for guidance. External sources have a limited view of reality, as their perceptions are based on what can be seen and touched. In addition, the guidance you get from others may conflict and be confusing to you as you strive to make informed, potentially life-altering decisions. This is because the advice you receive from others may be based on their own experiences and perceptions, which may not be aligned with your own.

Listen to all the well-intentioned advice and gauge it with your intuition, your gut feelings. Take what works for you and leave the rest behind. When it is right for you, it will ring true in your heart and your gut.

Ultimately, you must learn to trust your inner self—your inner compass—your innate GPS, to help you move through significant transitions and barriers, and to point you toward your next step. Trust your inner knowledge as it will guide you to the best path, even if those around you do not understand or you cannot even explain it yourself. Your insight uniquely suits your own situation, rather than other people's opinions or expectations.

While listening to your gut seems straightforward, most people ignore these feelings. Unfortunately, intuition does not always seem rational, and you may think you are overreacting or making too much of something because it rarely spells things out, giving instructions you can clearly understand.

In all cases, the messages are not always as clear or as easy to understand as we would like them to be, which is probably why many people do not follow their intuition. Even though the messages are not always clear, they can sometimes be repetitive, and that is when you need to pay attention to your intuition. Is there a persistent thought that keeps coming to mind, such as changing careers, feeling suspicious of someone, or other constant thought?

We are constantly being bombarded with intuitive messages in different forms. Sometimes it is a gut feeling when you know that something is not right or that something is about to happen, but you do not have any evidence to substantiate or define the feeling. Sometimes it can be an overwhelming feeling that you should be elsewhere, doing something, or avoiding a certain place or thing. Or it can be a fight-or-flight response that causes those little hairs on the back of your neck to stand up, to warn you that something bad is about to happen. Sometimes your intuition will deliver a message with words spoken through another person, a song, or situation and you just must be able to decipher the clues.

Even when you are distracted by day-to-day activities and challenges, your intuition, that little voice that we often ignore, is in the background guiding and encouraging you.

In the Summer of 2001, As the business development manager for the US, I was required to fly to Los Angeles at least once per month. My preferred itinerary to Los Angeles was to take the first flight out, which was American Airlines Flight 77.

Although this had been my routine for months, each month, I found myself looking for an excuse not to go to California. This apprehension puzzled me, as I had done extensive travel for both personal and business reasons. I did not know what to make of my reluctance to fly. My unwillingness to fly only surfaced when it came time to travel to California.

During the week of September 3, 2001, the senior manager of our business development group walked into my office to discuss the possibility that I would be reassigned to another department by the end of the month. Given this information, I planned to complete any ongoing negotiations but defer any renegotiations of new contracts to the person who would replace me.

Taking full advantage of a legitimate excuse to cancel my travel plans to Los Angeles, I contacted my counterparts and confirmed that they had no problem with postponing the timing of our renegotiations. I waited until Friday, September 7, to cancel my scheduled trip to Los Angeles, California.

Many of us remember exactly where we were and what we were doing when we heard of the attacks on the twin towers of the World Trade

Center in New York City on September 11, 2001. I stood among a crowd of colleagues frozen in place and silenced by the shock of the unfolding events.

As the American Airlines Boeing 767 crashed into the north tower around 8:45 a.m., I thought, "This has to be a terrorist attack." As I continued to watch in horror and disbelief, a United Airlines Boeing 767 appeared on the screen and crashed into the south tower, approximately eighteen minutes after the north tower crash. I was certain this was a terrorist attack. We later witnessed in horror as the towers collapsed and thousands lost their lives before our eyes.

As millions of Americans watched the unfolding events on their televisions, an American Airlines Boeing 757 crashed into the west side of the Pentagon in Washington, DC.

If the senior manager of our group had not come into my office that afternoon to discuss the possibility of reassignment, I would have been on American Airlines Flight 77 on September 11, 2001, and part of the devastating inferno and rubble that killed 125 Pentagon employees plus the airline passengers.

When I first heard the newscast, I did not make an immediate connection, as it would not have taken a little over an hour for an airplane to get from Washington Dulles Airport to the Pentagon in Washington DC.

It wasn't until I heard the actual details that I finally made the connection. The airplane that crashed into the Pentagon was the same flight I took each month to travel to Los Angeles and the one I had canceled four days earlier. It took me a few weeks to get past the surreal feeling of disbelief and begin fully processing what had transpired. The magnitude of the unfolding events of the previous week did not immediately sink in.

Each time I had crossed the threshold and boarded American Airlines Flight 77, I had always had an ominous and foreboding feeling. It was like a warning of something to come, and I hadn't known what to make of it until the incident on September 11, 2001.

Besides the foreboding feelings, the actions of the senior manager of our group, who was not my direct supervisor, were perplexing. I still can't explain it. There were two levels of management between us, and the responsibility for advising me of any potential career move rested with my direct supervisor, not the senior manager. My interaction with the senior manager was so strange and out of character that I didn't even share the conversation with my direct supervisor.

After I fully understood the events of September 11, I saw the discussion with the senior manager as divine intervention. Not only did I not move to the other department, but I also didn't hear another word about a potential move from anyone. Nor did I ask. At that point, it was irrelevant.

The primary purpose of the conversation with the head of our unit had been to keep me off of the American Airlines flight on that fateful day. The universe had known that I would take any excuse presented to me to cancel my trip to California. Fortunately, I had listened to my intuition.

I had been receiving intuitive flashes of insight that had been warning me about something to come on this flight for months. Although I couldn't have predicted the events that transpired on September 11, the message had been clear that I needed to cancel my trip. This insight had protected me, as it had encouraged me to stay away.

Some might say it was not my time to go or explain it differently. But for me, this was divine intervention giving me the signals I needed to stay off of that fateful flight on September 11, 2001, through routine, daily workplace events that determined my fate.

A seemingly inconsequential decision to cancel a business trip made the difference between life and death for me.

You do not always have the luxury of time to sit down and analyze a situation, and it is, therefore, harder to make the right choice under pressure. In those situations, go with your intuition, your gut feelings. Several scientific studies have shown that a correct gut feeling can hit us before our brains can even rationally process what is going on. Think of the many times you ignored your gut feelings just to have them confirmed later.

Learn to trust your gut feelings and let your inner compass guide you along the way. There will be no neon signs pointing out directions or written rules to ensure your success. Like everything else in life, trusting your intuition and following its guidance takes practice.

The more you allow yourself to act upon your inner guidance, the easier it gets. At first, intuition may come in a flash as a fleeting insight, which you may dismiss as coincidence or your imagination.

Acknowledging your intuition will strengthen it and be more accurate.

Discovering Your Life's Purpose—Why Am I Here?

Do you feel unmotivated, unsure of yourself, aimless, directionless, and unclear of what you want out of life? Are you looking to lead a more meaningful life? A life that makes you want to jump out of bed excited to face the day's activities. If so, you are not alone; there are millions in the same position. We all have moments in our lives when we feel lost and uncertain about our next step. During these times of uncertainty, it is important to be true to yourself and follow your heart and gut feelings.

Before we are born, we collaborate with our guides to orchestrate a life mission and path. However, when we incarnate, we forget why we are here and spend a lot of time and energy trying to answer the question, "Why am I here?" We constantly search for clues that will help us decipher the journey of our soul. However, the rules of incarnation require that we would not remember absolutely anything about the path we will walk in this lifetime or the experiences in previous lifetimes. Thick veils fall over our consciousness, and we forget everything that we planned for our chosen path.

Forgetting our purpose in life is like briskly walking into a room with a specific purpose in mind. Then you stop abruptly because you do not remember what you were supposed to be doing in that room. Remembering your purpose in that room could take a few seconds, minutes, or a few days before you can recall.

Remembering our life purpose can be early in life. Some people seem to know exactly what they want or should do at an early age. As young adults, they know exactly what they want for a profession and diligently pursue their career. Some know that their purpose in life is to be a parent and they have children at an early age and devote their lives to rearing children, grandchildren, and keeping a home. For others, it can take years to figure out their soul's mission.

Your purpose encompasses your passion, your life's mission, your reason for being. Identifying your purpose takes time and commitment. A self-evaluation of your innate talents, abilities, and desires is required to get a sense of direction and to define your passion.

No matter what you aspire for yourself, your family, or your career; your life's purpose will put you in the driver's seat and allow you to take control of your future. Having clear direction regarding your aspirations will minimize your chances of ending up haphazardly moving along a path that does not bring the reward, satisfaction, and achievement that you seek.

As you embark on the journey to find your life's purpose, remain flexible and courageous. Embracing significant life changes and taking risks may lead to failures, but these setbacks are merely the experiences necessary for your soul's growth. Have no fear of moving out of your comfort zone into unknown territory. Do not let the fear of failure prevent you from pursuing your dreams. To achieve your greatest aspirations, exhibit the courage to take risks and explore unfamiliar territory, which may mean facing difficult situations that are unsuccessful.

As your life's purpose is unfolding, you may drift away from the people you used to identify with, even your family. This is just part of the process.

When something captures our attention, it is giving us information; it is a shame that we ignore those signals and their meaning. Have faith in the messages your intuition is sending you. Trusting the messages you receive is essential. At first, the messages will not be as clear or easy to decipher. But as you continue to exercise the intuition muscle, it will get stronger. Be patient with yourself, as this will not happen overnight. Realizing your goals, whether financial, educational, health, weight, or something else may seem daunting, overwhelming, and elusive. It may be difficult to remain optimistic when you see no evidence of your dreams coming to fruition. However, you must continue to believe in yourself, regardless of negative circumstances and input from those around you.

Your dreams may require time, energy, or other action on your part before they materialize. Stay positive, be optimistic, and keep plugging away at your important goals. Chances are you are doing much better than you think, and success is most likely just around the corner.

The key to living a full life is to recognize and make the most of your strengths. Take the time to figure out what you are good at, what comes naturally to you, the skills you have mastered, and a rewarding life will follow.

Few individuals have the privilege of pursuing their passion as a profession. For most people, this opportunity arises only after they have retired or are independently wealthy and do not have to work for a living. However, that does not have to stop us from trying to identify what we love to do, what may put us in a good mood, what we get complimented for, what makes our hearts sing with joy. You may not know what you are looking for, but you will recognize your passion and purpose when you discover it.

At first there will be nothing but a simmering glow of a dream. The glow waxes and wanes as your doubts and fears keep it from surfacing from its hiding place somewhere deep inside your mind. Your believing makes you feel empowered to make that dream a reality. As you plan the execution of your dream, you will start visualizing pictures of your dream coming alive and you will then be able to take your passion and make it happen.

As you reflect on your life, is there something that you have voiced that you want to do? Is there something that everyone points out to you that you do very well and would make an ideal profession for you? Is there something that has always fascinated you? What activity or initiative would you engage in even if you didn't receive payment?

As I reflected on my life, I recognized that writing was something I had always wanted to do. Since the early 1990s, I'd been saying that I was going to write a book about my maternal grandparents lives. However, raising a family, career, and educational pursuits did not give me the luxury to sit down and do some creative writing.

I prepared for the future book by asking my mother questions about her life as a child, her father, and her mother. I listened intently and took copious notes. I started seriously writing and researching in 2000 as a hobby. I'd work on the manuscript sporadically whenever I had the time and inspiration.

I even took a creative writing course at Northern Virginia University and was so discouraged by the professor's comments on my writing ability and style. that I put the manuscript down for about four years. What made me think I could write a book? But despite the negative experience, that nagging voice in my head kept telling me I had to write and publish this book.

In 2012, I self-published *Empower Yourself for an Amazing Career* as a practice book to get a glimpse of the publishing world. In this book, I share career advice, drawing heavily from my corporate career. In 2019, after I retired and my kids were independent, I published *Pursuing a Better Tomorrow* about 30 years from the time I started talking and thinking about it. The book morphed into so much more than my maternal grandparents stories. The book spans more than one hundred years, which portrays the history of three generations, and is an inspiring cross-generational journey from Spain to New York City. The memoir's four interconnected stories focus on one of the main characters in a given era. Their personal stories illustrate the challenges and opportunities of immigration, acculturation, coming of age, and self-discovery through the characters' psychological and moral growth. The characters portray the strength of character required to achieve a better tomorrow given the twists, turns, and synchronistic events that shaped their lives.

This illustrates my point that sometimes all there is a simmering glow of a dream and then one day it comes to fruition. I knew that writing was something I wanted to do but not in the quest to become an author.

Notwithstanding that I was not an author, I've always been fascinated by the written word. I grew up hearing a lot of sayings (clichés) and always had fun getting down to the meaning or lesson that the phrase delivers. When I discover the inspiration or wisdom behind the words, I get that Aha! Moment that leads to profound thinking. For example, the simple cliché 'walk a mile in another's shoes.' Those six words say so much about not being judgmental, criticizing another's actions and motives, and being more tolerant. I am fascinated by the art of creation, inspiration, empowerment of the written word and will continue to write even if no one reads what I write.

In this book, I use clichés and pair with a short story or idea that gets to the wisdom and message of the phrase. Editors hate clichés but I love them as they are succinct and get to the heart of the matter and point in a brief phrase.

Reflect on your passions and interests: What makes you come alive? What are you naturally drawn to? Reflecting on your passions and interests can give you clues about your purpose and the direction of your soul's journey. Once you have a sense of your purpose and direction, take action towards your goals. This can be in small steps or gigantic leaps, but the important thing is to keep moving toward your goals.

Identifying your life's purpose is like solving a mystery, one clue at a time. Through introspection, you will decipher the clues and put all the pieces together until Voilà a light bulb goes off in your head and you identify your purpose.

Choose Your Own Path

From the moment we are born, we are guided and told what to do, how to do it, when to do it, and why we need to do it. Our lives are led by the rules imposed on us by our parents, teachers, societal norms, religion, or other entities. As children and young adults, we are expected to follow those rules and limitations without ever questioning them. However, when we grow into adulthood, it is up to us to choose our individual path regardless of how we were raised and what we were exposed to as a child.

When we find ourselves at crossroads in life, we may go back to some of those rules imposed on us. But we also must look within and tap into our inner GPS to help us navigate the scary road taking a risk, and not turning your back or just following the crowd or what someone else has told you to do.

Well-intentioned friends and family may try to influence you to do things their way. However, if you ignore your inner voice and listen to others, you will become resentful and lose your sense of identity and purpose.

Regardless of our upbringing, we recognize and embark on our chosen path when we become adults. Once we embark on our unique path, we rarely question its rightness or wrongness because we just know it feels right and aligns with our purpose in this lifetime. Your inner guidance will help you identify your passions and emphasize the benefits of not following the crowd and choosing your own path. Your inner guidance will give you the courage to follow your chosen path even if it is difficult.

The one thing many famous and successful people have in common is that they carved their own path in life no matter the odds of success or what other people thought. They didn't want to be just another person in the crowd; they wanted to be unique, one of a kind in their chosen field.

It is easy to follow the crowd and have someone tell you exactly what to do, but that does nothing for your self-development and will only delay you from leading the life you were born to lead. The sooner you can identify and embark on your path, the sooner you will start living the life you were born to live.

Free Will and Co-creation in Spiritual Contexts

Free Will refers to the ability to make choices that are not predetermined by past events or divine intervention. It's the idea that from the moment we are born, we can make decisions that shape our lives.

Co-creation is the process by which our choices and actions collaborate with the universe or a higher power to manifest our reality. It suggests that when we consciously choose our experiences for learning and growth, we actively take part in shaping our journey.

We handpick the experiences we wish to have for learning the life lessons we want to explore. By doing so wisely, we enter a state of co-creation where things seem simpler because we are in alignment with our true desires and the flow of the universe.

Our inner radiance is our life force. It's the energy we channel into every decision we make. This energy, which we often refer to as 'light,' becomes conscious of its might when we recognize that this inner glow is, in its most advanced form, is the very core of our divine nature. Our inner light is our most valuable resource; the core of our being—our spirit or essence—is the ultimate guide in our decisions. This inner light, or intuition, helps us navigate life and is in sync with the mysterious laws of co-creation. It suggests that by listening to our inner guidance, we can make choices that resonate with our soul's purpose and contribute to the creation of our reality. This inner light influences all your decisions and harmonizes with the enigmatic principles of co-creation. It encourages us to recognize and use our inherent power of choice and to understand that we are not passive observers but active participants in the unfolding of our lives. It aligns with spiritual growth and the belief in the power within, highlighting the importance of self-awareness and the conscious direction of one's life path.

To fully embrace our chosen path and truly 'live,' additional forces must come into play. We often perceive energy as originating from an external source. However, if one is truly authentic, the opposite is true—you are the source of your energy. This energy stems from the infinite cosmos, and we are just a small part of it, embodied in a physical body. Recognizing this subtle shift empowers you to understand that the power lives within you. You are a divine entity in its entirety. At this very moment, you can manifest all that you desire and shape your own 'reality.' Grant yourself the permission to dream big dreams for both the world and yourself and watch as they materialize.

Your inner essence is the most precious asset you possess on this planet. It's not the quantity of your possessions that matters, but the intentions behind your acquisitions. Similarly, it's not the actions themselves that define you, but the reasons for those actions, your intentions.

In the realm of energy, there are no hidden truths; everything is clear and known. This reflects a spiritual perspective on energy and truth. It suggests that in the energetic realm, unlike the physical world, there are no secrets or concealed motives; everything is transparent and observable. This viewpoint aligns with the belief that our intentions and choices are energetically expressed and understood, even if they are not outwardly apparent.

Every decision you make and the motivations behind them are visible, as our innermost thoughts and feelings are perceptible on an energetic level. It's a reminder that authenticity and self-awareness are important, as we cannot truly hide our intentions. Thus, the law of cause and effect refers to the principle that every action has a corresponding reaction. In spiritual teachings, this is often related to the idea of karma, where the choices we make have consequences that shape our experiences.

The adage "the truth will set you free" is a timeless piece of wisdom that encourages honesty and integrity. It implies that embracing and living your truth creates a path to freedom and liberation from falsehood and illusion. The adage also resonates with the journey towards enlightenment and the understanding that our actions and intentions have profound effects on our lives and the world around us. It's a call to live with transparency and to recognize the interconnectedness of our decisions and their effects on our lives that of others.

Negative Energy

The concept of negative energy is often used in a metaphorical sense to describe the impact of certain behaviors or attitudes that can affect one's mood or environment. While not a scientific term, it's a way people express the draining or unpleasant feelings they experience in the presence of certain individuals or situations.

Dealing with individuals who seem to radiate negative energy can be challenging. It's important to remember that everyone has their own struggles and reasons for their behavior. This doesn't mean you have to accept negativity, but understanding this can help you protect your own energy and respond appropriately. A few strategies that may help when interacting with negativity:

- **Set Boundaries:** Decide what you are and aren't willing to tolerate and set boundaries to protect your own well-being.
- **Stay Positive:** Focusing on solutions rather than problems can counter negativity.
- **Empathy:** "walk a mile in someone else's shoes." Try to put yourself in the other person's shoes. It's hard to decipher why people do what they do but trying to understand where they're coming from and showing compassion can go a long way.
- **Self-Care:** Engage in activities that boost your mood and keep you grounded.
- **Limit Exposure:** If possible, minimize the time spent with those who drain your energy.
- **Seek Support:** Talk to friends or professionals who can offer advice and support.

You can't control the action of others, but you can control how you respond to them. Following your own path requires that you be honest with yourself. You may have to move away from familiar places and groups as you embark on your own path. Initially, it may feel lonely, and you may think you made a mistake. However, be patient and you'll find like-minded people that will support your goals. The miracles that each of us can perform are infinite. We can each improve the quality of our lives tenfold by just homing in on our inner power.

Spiritual guides say that "nothing happens by accident or sheer coincidence." Everything happens exactly when it is supposed to, not a minute earlier. So, you will figure out your purpose in this lifetime. Only you can determine the ultimate path that you will travel.

Understand your purpose and your potential so that you can take control of your emotions, your life, and your future. You can choose to do good or evil, work hard or be lazy, be happy or sad, and the universe will compensate you accordingly. The law of cause and effect, which balances all experiences, shows that in the end, everyone gets what they deserve. Life operates on the principle of cause and effect, where our actions have consequences or balancing of our experiences. I like to refer to life as a zero-sum game where you reap what you sow.

It may appear to be difficult, maybe even impossible, but nothing is going to change the path you chose for your soul to travel. There is nothing to impede the realization of your dreams and the desires in your heart because these are part of your soul's mission—the path you chose to walk in this lifetime. *"No one can build you the bridge on which you, and only you, must cross the river of life." — Friedrich Nietzsche*

Your Soul's Journey

Your path is unique to you. Your soul's journey is an individual experience that is exclusive to you. Indeed, there are those individuals who enter and exit your life as characters in the movie of your life. Certain people stay in your life forever, while other relationships are short-lived. Life has a way of bringing us the right people at the perfect time. People will come in and out of your life. When a relationship ends, it means that it has served its purpose. While we can mourn the loss of a relationship, it simply signifies that it is time to move on to a new experience.

You set the priorities in your life by your thoughts and the universe helps you manifest thoughts into reality. Your life expresses the thoughts you choose to manifest. The people, events, and circumstances that show up in your life result from the thoughts and intentions you have launched in the past. If you launch new thoughts and intentions now, then new people, events, and circumstances will show up to reflect your updated frame of mind and view of life.

You are the architect of your destiny, choosing specific aspects and themes for your life. The decisions you make will ultimately shape who you are as a person. This journey is an in-depth exploration of who you are, revealing facets of your genuine identity and purpose. We decide about certain areas of our lives before we incarnate. The path you chose is paved by every decision and experience you have. This journey shapes who we are in this lifetime and is inextricably linked to your former lifetimes.

Good and evil need to coexist, and this coexistence is definitely a fascinating aspect of our existence. This duality echoes through various philosophical and spiritual traditions. In many belief systems, the contrast between positive and negative forces is essential for growth, learning, and transformation. For example:

Yin and Yang (Taoism): In Taoist philosophy, the concept of yin and yang represents the dualistic nature of existence. Yin (the dark, receptive, and feminine) and Yang (the bright, active, and masculine) are complementary opposites. They coexist and create balance.

Christianity: The story of Jesus and Judas exemplifies this idea. Judas, despite his betrayal, played a crucial role in the unfolding of events leading to Jesus' crucifixion and resurrection. The story of Jesus is incomplete without Judas. Judas' betrayal brings into sharp contrast the luminous themes of redemption and forgiveness.

Reincarnation and Karma: The belief in reincarnation suggests that souls experience multiple lifetimes, taking on various roles and learning lessons along the way. Karma, the law of cause and effect, implies that our actions have consequences. We reap what we sow, whether positive or negative.

Evolution of consciousness: The concept of evolution of consciousness suggests that our souls develop through life's experiences. The various roles we assume—whether as a victim, offender, healer, or educator—enhance our soul's progression. It is through embracing these diverse perspectives that we cultivate qualities like empathy, compassion, and insight.

These perspectives are symbolic and metaphorical. Whether you view them as literal truths or powerful allegories, they invite us to explore the complexity of existence.

We incarnate in pods with the same people playing different roles. We experience multiple lifetimes, taking on various roles. This cycle of participation in different roles is crucial to the evolution of our souls. These are people that have shared their lives with you. Your travel partners on your journey coincide in different existences in different lifetimes. Whoever is your child in this lifetime could be your brother, grandchild, or any other member of your family in another lifetime. Every being that crosses your path does so for a specific reason and these people leave an indelible imprint on your soul contributing to your evolution.

The idea of incarnating in pods and playing different roles for the evolution of the soul is the interconnectedness and the cyclical nature of existence. In this cosmic theater, we each take our turn on the stage, donning various masks and costumes. Sometimes we're the hero, other times the villain, and occasionally the silent observer. Each role contributes to our growth, understanding, and empathy. It is through these diverse experiences that our souls expand and evolve.

Life, with all its twists and turns, becomes a grand tapestry woven from countless threads of existence. We learn, we love, we stumble, and we rise again. And as we play our part, we unknowingly influence others, leaving an indelible mark on their journeys as well.

This idea, whether it aligns with spiritual beliefs or serves as a metaphor, is thought-provoking. So, let's continue our participation in the cosmic theater, embracing the roles we assume, knowing that each step enriches the grand composition of existence.

The process of choosing the path we will walk in each lifetime is akin to selecting a film at the cinema, deciding whether it will be an adventure, a drama, or any genre we desire. We opt to purchase a ticket for our chosen experience. When we immerse ourselves in a film about forbidden love, we empathize with the characters, weep alongside them, and are swept up by a torrent of emotions. We yearn to experience these emotions—disdain, hatred, vengeance and the opportunity to experience the full spectrum of human emotions is the fundamental reason for our journey through various life cycles.

When contemplating our existence and the journey of our souls, the concept of life and death becomes deeply intertwined. Each person's beliefs and perspectives on this matter can vary significantly, but there's a universal fascination with the transition from life to whatever lies beyond.

In the grand tapestry of existence, we weave our own threads. It's the idea that our lives are like a grand tapestry, and each of us contributes to its creation through our choices, experiences, and relationships. These elements come together to form patterns that represent our individual journeys.

Our choices, experiences, and connections form intricate patterns that define our unique paths. We shape our destiny, whether consciously or unconsciously suggesting that our actions and decisions significantly affects the course of our lives. This concept is embraced in various forms across different cultures and spiritual beliefs, from the idea of "karma" in Hinduism and Buddhism to the concept of the "Book of Life" in Abrahamic religions.

Whether it involves beliefs in reincarnation, an afterlife, or other spiritual ideologies, the underlying message is that we play an active role in our own spiritual evolution. This aligns with your interest in understanding the human experience and the significance of personal growth and self-discovery.

This spiritual belief encourages self-awareness and mindfulness, reminding us we are the architects of our fate and that every moment is an opportunity to weave beauty, meaning, and purpose into the tapestry of our existence. It's a perspective that resonates with many as it empowers individuals to take ownership of their spiritual journey.

Your soul's journey is about your ongoing evolution and growth through multiple incarnations accumulating and comprehending the events you experience. It's experiencing, learning, changing, and evolving. The true meaning of the soul's journey is defined by your choices and actions to define and mold it. The concept of your soul's journey is vast and extends far beyond the limitations of a single lifetime. It includes the many incarnations and experiences your soul has had during previous lifetimes.

This journey connects your life in the spirit realm with your physical incarnations. We choose specific aspects of our lifetime while in the spirit realm and then walk that path in our physical incarnation. Your soul goes through this continuous process as it transforms into a fully formed, competent, creative being. Every soul's journey is unique, distinguished by its own decisions, experiences, and lessons, as opposed to a set path. This is your unique journey of self-discovery and spiritual growth.

As we incarnate into the various lifetimes, the primary goal of each incarnation is to transform and evolve. The evolution of a lifetime is a constant learning experience and despite previous lifetimes it is at first difficult to see the way forward. However, little by little, we learn how to trust our inner guidance. Living in alignment with our soul's purpose can bring a deep sense of fulfillment and joy, even in the face of challenges and setbacks. We can be anything we want if we allow ourselves to follow our chosen path. We can be anything we dream we could be by imagining and manifesting our dreams into reality. It is a matter of changing the way we think and being impeccable with our thoughts. *"Imagination is everything. It is the preview of life's coming attractions."* ⊠ *Albert Einstein*

Human beings incarnate with a specific purpose and path for their souls to travel. This is your path, your soul's journey, not your parents. Parents cannot take full credit or full blame for how their children turn out. Children come into this world with their own agenda. Parents are merely the catalyst that helped them enter this world.

"Your vision will become clear only when y ou investigate your heart. He who looks outside, dreams. He who looks inside, awakens."
— Carl Jung

CHAPTER 3

WALKING THE WALK OF YOUR CHOSEN PATH

"Remember to follow your own true path, your way to the top. Don't let anyone stop you, not even a flop."
—**Ari Gunzburg**

Walking the walk of your chosen path is metaphorical. However, the twists and turns of life can be likened to traversing a winding trail, a rocky road, a brick road, or a smoothly paved road with footsteps echoing along the way.

On your chosen path, each step becomes a decision, a commitment to the direction you've chosen. This metaphorical walk through life is the profound act of moving forward and discovering your path. Your chosen path is a way of life that you have decided for this lifetime. So, walk your walk with purpose and with the quiet determination of someone forging ahead despite obstacles.

Embracing our roles in life is a multifaceted process that involves self-discovery, acceptance, and growth. Below are some things that may ease your walk down your chosen path.

- Self-Acceptance—Embrace Your Uniqueness
- Project Confidence—Boost Your Self-Esteem
- Master Your Fears
- Shake Off the Bitterness
- Lean on Someone
- Embrace New Beginnings

These focal points are not meant to be all-inclusive, and one size certainly does not fit all. Take the ones that work for you and leave the rest behind. I also encourage you to find a specific focus that will support you as you pursue your chosen path. Life is a journey, and focusing on these points can guide you to a more fulfilling and purposeful life.

Self-Acceptance—Embrace Your Uniqueness

"Be who you are and say what you feel, because those who mind don't matter, and those who matter don't mind."
— **Dr. Seuss**

You are unique and there is no one else on this earth exactly like you, whether it is your sense of fashion, style, humor, or manner of speaking that makes you unique. If your way produces a positive outcome, be proud of it, even if it does not conform to the mainstream. Learn to discover, embrace, and express your individuality. Your uniqueness makes you who you are; and when you try to be something you are not or something you do not feel comfortable with, you only lose your identity.

Whenever you indulge in denying or hiding any aspect of your true self, it is the equivalent to rejecting yourself. We all want to be included and accepted by others, but how do you expect to be accepted, loved, and appreciated by others when you do not even accept yourself? You need to accept yourself first, then others will follow suit.

There is no escape from yourself. There is nowhere to hide. You cannot live life to its fullest if you are constantly shrinking away, trying to hide the parts of yourself that are not comfortable. To continue growing as a person and extract maximum value out of life, we must expose the good, the bad, and the ugly. We need to embrace the possibility of errors and the courage to venture into the unknown.

Look within and honestly identify the aspects of yourself that you are hiding or striving to change. Is there some physical, emotional, or other apparent or perceived flaw you feel you just cannot live with? Is this your true feeling? Alternatively, could it be that you are simply reflecting what you think others find unacceptable and you want to conform by denying and repressing feelings or judging yourself too harshly?

Imagine for one moment that you accepted and liked everything about yourself, including—physical qualities, personality traits, the way you interact with others, your gifts, and talents. How does this self-acceptance feel?

Bring to your full awareness the things you dislike about yourself. Is there anything you can do to change them? If not, introduce yourself to this perceived deficiency, embrace it as part of your uniqueness, and acknowledge its presence in your life without judgment.

Your unique energy and purpose are expressed through your talents, passions, and vision. When you are in touch with your true self and act upon your inner guidance, your life will be much more rewarding and fulfilling, and you will live with a sense of purpose.

You must accept yourself for the wonderful person you are. Accept that you are just as important as everyone else in your midst. We all have a different purpose in life, and your goals and objectives are just as important as the next person's goals.

Invest in your uniqueness. Your investment counselor, your inner self, has infinite resources and is constantly laying many gifts and blessings at your doorstep. All you need to do is open the door to all the possibilities.

What makes you unique? Do not be afraid to exhibit and capitalize on your uniqueness. That unique, innate skill or strength may just be the one thing that could help you achieve your goals and objectives.

Identify those activities or skill set that come naturally to you and seem to come from somewhere deep inside yourself. Do you know your strengths and weaknesses? We all have a range of natural abilities, some things that come easy to us. These may be things we do because we are good at them or because other people value them and pay us to do them. This talent is uniquely yours because even though others may have the same ability, no one can deliver results exactly like you. Your unique combination of personal traits and life experiences makes your style unique to you, and no one will affect others in quite the same way.

Self-acceptance is an inside job. When you fear looking at your true self, you will find many ways to distract yourself. Sometimes, this could lead to addictions or other unacceptable behavior. However, to find your identity and accept who you are you must stop running from yourself and accept who you were born to be. Get to know the real You and start living the life you were born to live and walk your chosen path. Self-expression is the key ingredient to reaching your full potential. When you live true to yourself, you avoid becoming frustrated and depressed. Bottling up your true self can lead to the loss of your identity and cause you to become exasperated, frustrated, and depressed as you lose your sense of self. Expressing the truth about yourself can help you get back on track and avoid losing your self-identity.

Learning to accept and re-affirm your true, powerful position in life and remold your thinking will end your self-sabotaging behavioral patterns. New, empowering thoughts will yield the benefit of knowing that life has equipped you with everything you need to succeed.

When you find yourself in distress or conflict, resist the urge to judge or criticize yourself. Instead, get in touch with your true self. Judgment, punishment, and power plays tend to further separate people from their true self and encourages self-defeating behavior.

Indulging in self-pitying thoughts and emotions is destructive. Take the time to identify and heal all insecurities. Stop being your own worst enemy and harshest critic.

Self-acceptance is critical. Practice self-acceptance by making yourself aware of all your perceived deficiencies and stop judging yourself. If you find yourself judging your uniqueness, stop and change your mind-set to one of acceptance; allow yourself to be unique. Shine your true essence onto all the parts you previously rejected and notice how this lifts you up and supports you in being freer and authentic.

When you embrace and accept yourself, the world will also accept you "as is." The acceptance you receive or don't receive from others reflects your own self-acceptance. If you feel sad or frustrated because you are not respected, accepted, appreciated, or acknowledged by those around you, it is really a reflection of your own feelings. You are confusing self-acceptance with acceptance from others.

You do not have to force or manipulate others to love, accept, respect, and honor you. Your self-respecting and accepting attitude will proceed from within you and you will focus less on what others think.

You will drift away from those that do not match your opinion of yourself and grow closer to those that match and honor your inner guidance.

You cannot depend on the opinion of others to define yourself because not everyone is going to like or accept you. If you try to conform to the opinion of others, you will grow confused and lose your identity as you struggle to be something you are not.

Reclaim your personal power. Do not give your power away. You must stand up for yourself now and then, lest folks take advantage of you and your ability to get easily offended.

Too many of us whine and complain about how other people mistreat us, but we never stand up to those bullies. It is okay to discuss the issue with someone that will help you develop a plan for dealing with the offender, but you must then have the courage to implement the plan. So instead of being overly sensitive and easily offended, take action to rectify the situation.

However, if for whatever reason you cannot rectify the situation, then you need to distance yourself from that person or situation. If you cannot distance yourself, learn to ignore and let it roll off your back.

Do not allow anyone to rob you of your personal power and break your spirit. Set boundaries and do not permit anyone who wants to drag you down to cross the boundary of disrespect. Defend yourself and do not let anyone break your spirit and resolve. I recognize that in some situations this can be easier said than done. *"No one can make you feel inferior without your consent." ~ Eleanor Roosevelt* Radiate, emit confidence, and self-acceptance and you will attract relationships that mirror and honor your true feelings.

Shower yourself with love, joy, and respect. Self-acceptance is an inside job.

> *"The world accommodates you for fitting in,*
> *but only rewards you for standing out."*
> **— Matzshona Dhilway**

Project Confidence—Boost Your Self Esteem

*"What you think of me is none of my business.
One of the highest places you can get to is being independent of the
good opinions of other people."*
— Dr. Wayne Dyer

You need to project confidence and never think that you are not as good as or as smart as the people around you because of your cultural background or education. Have faith in your skills and abilities and do not allow the opinion of others affect your self-confidence.

Self-confidence is how you feel about your abilities and can vary from situation to situation. Certain individuals seem to have innate self-confidence, while most people need to cultivate it. It is possible to nurture and grow self-confidence. However, getting it right is a matter of striking a perfect balance between low-confidence and over-confidence that is realistic and represents your true ability.

Boost your self-esteem. Self-esteem develops from experiences and situations that have shaped how you view yourself and it refers to how you feel about yourself overall.

Your self-perception is largely influenced by external perspectives. Negative self-perceptions that have been projected onto you by individuals who do not know or love themselves and lack self-awareness and self-acceptance.

Early in life, you believed you had deficiencies, to where you believed them, and tried to hide your true self for fear of being ridiculed.

Do not allow anyone's negative programming to cause you to lose your self-esteem or self-worth. Unfortunately, whether intentional or unintentional, some relationships shape and ingrain a negative reflection of self into our consciousness through years of disappointments, uncertainties, and doubt. They stay with us and form our overall perception of ourselves and life.

What do you see when you look in the mirror? There are two mirrors, there is the physical mirror, and the emotional mirror and what you see depends on which mirror you are focusing on.

We have heard quotes such as, "Beauty is personified from the inside," and "Beauty is in the eye of the beholder," meant to make someone feel better about their appearance.

Within the family, I felt like an outsider, as if I had been born into the wrong family, questioning whether I was adopted. But since that was not the case, then I can only surmise that I must've been born into the wrong family.

My looks, demeanor, and personality were opposed to the rest. Feeling different from others made me retreat into a world of my own, where I carefully planned my way out and waited for the perfect opportunity.

As a young woman, my mother was gorgeous with her European features and the Spanish Señorita look. My sister looked a lot like my mother—not as pretty, but you could tell where she had gotten her looks. My brother looked a lot like my paternal grandfather: fair-skinned, with blond hair and European features—a young Clint Eastwood look-alike. In fact, we called him Clint.

Then there was me. I was a shy, solemn child who rarely smiled. Any time anyone views any of my childhood pictures, they always ask, "Why were you so mad?" I swear I wasn't mad; it was the way I usually looked. In hindsight, the pictures depict an unhappy child. I had a flat nose, a huge ass, and buck teeth, and I wore thick coke-bottle glasses. To top it off, I had unruly curly hair with a mind of its own. Curly hair was not fashionable; it was long and straight hair or an afro. If ever I tried to straighten out the curls to appear more fashionable, my rebellious hair would frizz, refusing to be tamed. Yikes!

During those awkward adolescent years, I heard people—family and nonfamily alike—commenting on how unattractive I was and how I looked nothing like my sister.

I came to believe and internalize that I was ugly, indeed. It was impossible for me to find anything beautiful about myself. After all, the surrounding adults had reinforced that sentiment, so it had to be true. Didn't it? I had to embrace it, accept it, and move on.

To this day, whenever anyone pays any semblance of a compliment about my looks or appearance, I feel as if the person is ridiculing me. I think, "Surely it can't be true. They are just trying to be polite." For a long time, the image I saw when I looked in the mirror was that of a hideous girl whose lips were too fat, and nose was too flat. To this day, that ugly girl appears in the mirror from time to time.

I sensed that my mother was troubled by my appearance. When we were taking our passport pictures in Santo Domingo, I recall my mother telling me to gather my lips. As a six-year-old, I thought, 'how do I do that'? Although unsure 'how' to do it, I understood my lips had to be positioned to look smaller. I sucked in my lips, which resulted in a pissed off look in our passport picture. One other time when I was about eleven years old, my mother commented that you must be careful whom you marry, because you will have children who are not good-looking, and you will be embarrassed when you introduce them to your friends. I can't be 100 percent sure, but I had a feeling my mother was talking about me. After all, I was the ugly duckling of the family.

The first person to tell me they thought I was beautiful was my then boyfriend and later husband when I was about fifteen years old. I would say to him, "The only reason you see me as beautiful is that you love me, and we all know that love is blind."

How could I go through years of programming and not be affected by it, whether or not I wanted to be? The experience had verbally and emotionally diminished me to a negative self-image. When someone came along and acknowledged my worth, beauty, and value, I did not believe them.

Through that experience, I learned that, whether or not intentional, some relationships shape and ingrain a negative reflection of self into our consciousness through years of verbal abuse and destructive criticism. As an adult, I can attest that these negative reflections stay with us and develop our overall impressions of ourselves and life.

Fortunately, I have always been a practical and resilient person, even as a child. The comments were initially hurtful to me, but after a while, I learned to live with being comfortable in my skin. Embracing my blended African/European/Native roots, my brown skin, curly hair, flat nose, and other imperfections with a sense of pride. I had to accept, respect, and love myself first before I could expect anyone else to do so.

Additionally, I can attest from personal experience that being excessively worried about others' perceptions of oneself can have detrimental effects on one's psychological well-being and self-esteem. The best you can do is to be yourself, whatever that means to you, and everything else will fall into place. The constant worry about how you look and how others perceive you is a colossal waste of time and energy. There were more productive ways to spend my time.

Sometimes I look into the mirror and still see the ugly duckling, while other times I see the beautiful swan that the ugly duckling grew up to be.

Most children can't discern between constructive and destructive criticism and can be adversely affected by comments made by adults. "It's easier to build up a child than to repair an adult. *Your words and actions have power in your child's life. Use them wisely.*" — Unknown

It is human nature to experience an occasional secret fear that one is not good enough. You may feel that everyone else has it all together and that you are the only one struggling to keep it together. Don't let a false sense of self and the opinion of others affect your self-worth and self-esteem.

Being overly concerned with others' opinions can be limiting. While it's normal to be mindful of how you're seen by others, letting their judgments overly concern you can impede your self- improvement and happiness. Instead, cultivate a strong sense of self-worth that isn't easily shaken by others' opinions. Stay true to yourself and your values, rather than conforming to what you believe others expect. Also remember that everyone has their own opinions, and it's impossible to please everyone. We must always be willing to agree to disagree. Let go of the need for external validation. Instead, focus on the opinion of those who truly value you. Recognizing the difference between constructive and destructive criticism can go a long way. Ultimately, it's about finding a balance between being receptive to feedback and maintaining your own direction in life.

You can look up to people, but only if it is not at the expense of your own self-worth and self-esteem. Regard these people as your role models, people you want to learn from and emulate. And, as you grow in knowledge, strength, and status, stand beside them as your peers.

When you feel worthless and powerless, you sometimes attract circumstances, relationships, and situations that affirm that belief. Your body language will manifest your thoughts, and others will perceive your vulnerability and treat you as someone who does not deserve respect and can be pushed around. Replace those old insecurities and fears with new empowering thoughts and reclaim your self-worth and self-esteem so that you can realize the success you deserve.

Be presumptuous enough to believe that you are just as good as, as smart as, or better than those around you and that you have a significant contribution to make. Don't talk yourself out of greatness. Lord knows that there are probably plenty of people around you who are already working on that.

Let your true essence shine so that your soul can blossom like a flower in the springtime by displaying your genuine self and power. Do not allow yourself to fail by false ego, criticism of others, or false guilt.

Grow through the dirt despite the obstacles that have been placed in your path. Just as a plant pushes through the soil to reach the sunlight, we can overcome challenges and negativity to thrive. Through resilience and personal growth, you can choose to become stronger instead of being defeated. Each obstacle we face provides an opportunity to learn, adapt, and become more resilient. Growth isn't always linear. Sometimes it's messy, just like a plant pushing and growing through the dirt. With determination and resilience, you can rise above challenges and thrive.

Negativity from others can weigh us down, but we have the power to rise above it. Cultivating a positive mindset allows us to see challenges as steppingstones rather than stumbling blocks. Surround yourself with people who uplift you, encourage your growth, and believe in your potential. Distance yourself from negative people and environments.

Always remember that self-confidence comes from within and is the key to living a fulfilling life. Embrace your unique qualities and let your confidence shine!

> *"Because one believes in oneself, one doesn't try to convince others. Because one is content with oneself, one doesn't need others' approval. Because one accepts oneself, the whole world accepts him or her."*
> **—Lao Tzu**

Master Your Fears

"The fears we don't face become our limits."
—Robin Sharma

One emotion that we all have in common is that of fear. This emotion can hold us back from our own happiness and can thwart our success. To free yourself from your fear, you must make a conscious decision to face and master your fears by effectively managing your perceptions.

Perception is defined as the "process by which individuals select, organize, and interpret the input from their senses to give meaning and order to the world around them." Reality is defined as "something that exists independently of ideas concerning it."

Your reality is created by beliefs and perceptions that are based on thoughts and feelings and you can choose your perceptions. When an unpleasant event occurs in your life, you have the choice to respond to it in a way that is consistent with your chosen path.

For example, you just experienced a major career failure after many years on the job. You can choose to see this as a tragic event that has obliterated your ego and self-esteem. You go into massive depression mode thinking how you will never get another job, be able to pay your bills, lose your home, and the fears continue to pile up. Alternatively, you can choose to see this event as the catalyst that inspires you to change your career to do something that you really enjoy. Is destiny pointing you in a different direction and offering an open door for you to walk through?

Whenever you feel trapped in fear or confusion, you are most likely responding to appearances, ego-based fears, and judging a book by its cover. Challenge yourself to dig deeper into the storyline of that book and find the lessons and gifts hidden between the lines.

You may not have control over the major events in your life, but you can certainly take control of how to respond to them. You have the power to shape your own reality through your beliefs about the situation.

A person's beliefs and perceptions can significantly shape their reality. Individuals construct their own understanding and knowledge of the world through experiencing things and reflecting on those experiences. What we believe to be true can influence how we perceive and interact with the world. Our beliefs can limit or expand our opportunities.

Our perceptions function as filters through which we interpret the world, which can alter our experience of reality. Our beliefs can also create self-fulfilling prophecies. If we expect certain outcomes, the universe delivers. A positive or negative attitude can influence the outcome of a situation based on how we choose to respond. Our perceptions can dictate our behaviors, which can shape the environment around us. While there are objective aspects of reality that are independent of us, our subjective interpretations play a crucial role in shaping our personal experience of the world. It's a powerful reminder of the importance of cultivating a positive mindset and being mindful of our perceptions.

There is a saying in Spanish, "Cada cabeza es un Mundo." meaning that each person's mind is like a separate universe, filled with unique thoughts, beliefs, and perceptions that shape their reality. It reflects the essence of individuality and subjectivity reminding us the diversity of the human experience and the personal worlds we each inhabit.

Your beliefs determine your perception—your perceptions dictate how you respond to events.—your response to those events which are based on your perceptions shapes your reality. You always have the option to re-evaluate your belief system to determine whether you need to change it so that you can positively influence your reality.

Your version of reality is your perception. What you believe to be true is only as true as your worldly experiences and perceptions; how you choose to perceive things is how they will come across to you. Negative perceptions develop your overall impression of yourself and life, limiting your experiences to what your ego-based fears allow.

The ego is shallow and fear-based, and its primary focus is all about "me." With this ego-based focus, you are bound to make your worst fears come true. Ego-based fears can be extremely powerful and control your mind. If your self-image is threatened, the ego diligently goes to work by partnering with fear, creating a pattern of fearful thoughts, perceptions, and ideas.

The ego's role is to help you clearly understand your individual needs, values, and goals in life, constantly reminding you of who you are supposed to be. As such, it is constantly evaluating and manipulating fear-based emotions, such as inadequacy, humiliation, and fear of failure. These fear-based emotions can drown you in a pool of your own negativity, as your thoughts remind you repeatedly of your weaknesses, powerlessness, and hopelessness.

You need to confront your fears and finally get over them. You need to learn to accept your fears as a normal part of your life and deal with them so you can end the debilitating effects. Your reaction, attitude, and perception of fear will either hold you back or propel you to new heights.

I had to overcome two significant fears: one mechanical and the other psychological.

When I lived in New York, driving was optional because public transportation was the primary mode of travel, so I wasn't an experienced driver. My husband always drove. When we moved to Virginia, there was no public transportation, and driving became the only option. Suddenly, I was thrust onto the road with little experience behind the wheel, and I had to overcome my fear of driving, especially on the freeway.

Although I could have taken local roads to get to work, I was determined to overcome my anxiety about driving on highways. Every day, I nervously faced the highway with its high speeds, heavy traffic, and the feeling of being trapped with no easy way to stop or exit. I recognized that my fear stemmed from a lack of confidence in my abilities to drive at high speeds and navigate complex highway systems. Understanding the root cause of my fear was crucial. Gradually, driving on the highway every day boosted my confidence until the fear was gone.

My other major fear emerged when I was relatively new to the corporate environment. I was elated when given the opportunity to work in the one of the most prestigious groups in our company. These jobs were typically reserved for MBA graduates from top business schools, highflyers on overseas assignments, and industry veterans. This group was extremely competitive, with a 'sink-or- swim' and 'every-man-for-himself' attitude. This assignment was a significant test of my abilities.

However, my elation didn't last long as I started comparing myself to those around me, feeling less confident about my abilities to do the job and compete with others. My cultural background and the fact that I hadn't completed my MBA made me believe I wasn't good enough. I felt inadequate with only three years of part-time graduate work from Pace University, surrounded by MBA graduates from Wharton, Duke, Harvard, and Cornell. I let their credentials affect my self-esteem and confidence.

I talked myself into believing that I wasn't good enough and that no one would want to hear what I had to say. However, I diligently continued to do my job, even if it meant working harder than everyone around me and being over prepared. Fortunately, my lack of confidence didn't last long as I started seeing some of these Ivy League MBA graduates struggle to survive in the tough, competitive trading-room environment. Some didn't have the killer instinct required to thrive in that dog-eat-dog world. They had Wharton, Duke, Harvard, and Cornell; I had Pace University, ten years of industry experience, and all the lessons from my life experiences, which had heightened my intuition and survival skills.

We all have fears and some of us manage these fears better than others. For some, and depending on their fear, this can be much easier said than done. Running away from or burying your fears will not make them go away, it may just make them bigger and harder to overcome.

Sometimes, fear helps keep us safe as it stops us from taking dangerous risks. However, too much fear can make you powerless and impede your progress. Facing your fears is essential to living the life you most want to lead.

By overcoming your fears, you can gain confidence in yourself. There is no way that any of us is going to be completely fearless, as there will be common problems and struggles in our daily lives. The fears I am referring to are the debilitating fears that paralyze you into inactivity, leaving you unable to overcome adversity.

Fear can be an intense emotion that can paralyze your ability to make pertinent decisions in your life. Most times, we can easily name our fear and can spout the benefits and concerns with a particular action. However, there are times we feel afraid and cannot quite understand the cause of the fear. It could be the unknown outcome of a situation, fear of failure, or even success. Fear of the unknown consequence of a future action can be difficult to overcome since you will not know the outcome until a situation comes to pass.

To overcome your fears, it is imperative that you identify and understand what you are afraid of. When you feel paralyzed by fear, stop, and think about your options. There are many resources available to you that can help you research various potential outcomes. You should talk to friends, family, search the web. It is much easier to prepare for the unknown once you understand the kinds of consequences you may be facing. Once you have identified the top three potential outcomes, develop a plan for overcoming any obstacles that you may have identified. This may be premature, but at least you will have thought through a plan to resolve any potential issue.

You can then feel proud of yourself for confronting and addressing your fears. It takes courage to commit the time and effort to move forward despite your fear. It does not matter if you cave in at the last minute and decide not to go through with the action. That just means that you must step back and reassess your plan and adjust your goals to something less threatening. It may take a series of steps to overcome your fear and gain the courage you need to achieve your desired outcome.

Stop looking into the rearview mirror of your life and leave your hurts and insecurities behind. Look straight ahead with your head held high and get excited about your goals and where you want to go so that life can affirm all that you were born to be and do. Grow beyond the painful experience and stop perpetuating the hurt by reliving it in your mind.

Face your fears head-on and remember that fear is often a mental barrier that can be overcome with courage and action. Life is about soaring beyond the limitations placed on us by society, family, even ourselves, so that when you come to the end of your life's journey, you will have no regrets about all those things you wish you had done. No regrets on the woulda, coulda, shoulda moments in your life.

> *"Fears are nothing more than a state of mind."*
> **— Napoleon Hill**

Shake Off the Bitterness

Resentment is like drinking poison and waiting for the other person to die."
— **Carrie Fisher**

When you are convinced, life has been unfair to you, shaking off the bitterness can be difficult. However, releasing a bitter experience changes your mindset to see the good instead of the bad. Holding on to resentment makes you an emotional hostage to the other person or the situation, and it consumes your energy, enthusiasm, and effectiveness. Do not allow yourself to become an emotional hostage. Change your mindset to see the good or the lesson learned from the experience.

Let go of all the grudges from deep within your mind and heart, and just let others be. Whatever wrongs have been done to you or you may have done to others, accept them and move on. Heal all emotional wounds inflicted by a friend or family member, which is often the most painful. Let it go feeling completely free and unbound. It's completely fine to keep certain people or situations out of your life, even if they are immediate family members. It's important to protect yourself from harm or exploitation. You deserve respect and refuse to be disrespected and treated as a doormat.

Letting go of the resentment will free you from the hostage situation. Choosing to forgive is a healthier option than holding onto resentment and experiencing the negative impact on your well-being. Free yourself of the mental hold this person or situation has imposed. If you do not let go, you will remain trapped in your own world of misery.

We all want to live a joy-filled, enthusiastic, exciting life with the satisfaction that we are doing something worthwhile. To achieve that successful life, you need to shake off the bitterness in your heart without being a doormat, paranoid, or letting others take advantage of you.

In the end, the only thing you can control is your attitude. When something unpleasant happens, you can treat yourself to an hour or a day or even a week's outrage about it, but then drop it and move on.

Moving on can be easier for some following relationship breakups, job layoff, rejection, or illness. The key is to focus on changing your attitude and mindset from victim to empowered individual.

Shaking off the bitterness is the best strategy as it is the only way to find the happiness you so desperately want. Too often, we hold on to what has happened to us. We are reluctant to let go of the pain and the hurt becomes part of our being as we grow addicted to pain.

Too many of us get addicted to the benefits of being hurt. You get a lot of attention and sympathy, and some may even pamper you because life has been unfair, and you have been mistreated.

This addiction eats away at us and steals our joy, happiness, and peace of mind. Past hurts can create feelings of bitterness, resentment, anger, and revenge. No matter what it is, let it go.

Too often, we keep our failures alive by replaying them over and over in our minds, renewing the anger, stewing over them, and talking to others about what has happened to us.

Some situations can be difficult to overcome, especially if you feel it has obliterated your ego and self-esteem. The death of a loved one, career failure, loss of a relationship, or any other life-altering event can be a brutally devastating blow that leaves you feeling completely spent and depressed. These experiences can feel like a personal attack on your psyche that cuts deep down inside, attacking every fiber of your being and soul.

You go through many emotions as you try to figure out what just hit you. You feel afraid and lost, because you cannot seem to identify with that person who has just failed or now feels abandoned and alone. Going through these emotions is natural, and to heal the situation, you must go through every stage of the grieving process, which often includes disbelief, fear, anger, blame, and shame.

The process is unique for every person, and some move through these emotions quickly, while others linger an inordinate amount of time on each emotion. You may move back and forth between a couple of cycles and back to the beginning, with each iteration lasting less time as you move more quickly through each cycle, until one day it is just a fleeting thought. The key is not to get stuck; to move on as quickly as possible. Lingering too long on these negative emotions can impede your progress.

After you are done with the grieving process and you are finally humbled into acceptance, you need to have the courage to face the hard truths of your new situation, pick yourself up, and move on with your life. This will require that you resist the continual urge to ask and try to figure out why this has happened to you. It is human nature to want to know, investigate, and understand what led to the situation. However, you should not waste too much time trying to figure out why something has happened to you. Chances are you may never know why. So, let it go. Move on with your life.

Your ego tells you that you would be safer if you remembered and held on to the past. However, any suffering that you hold in your awareness simply attracts more of the same hurtful situations. As such, it is imperative that you cut the strings that keep you attached to painful memories so that you stop attracting more of the same.

The key is to accept what has happened, try to make sense out of it, learn from it, and then let it go. When you let it go, you feel free and no longer a hostage to the situation.

The decision to move on is entirely up to you and the sooner you let it go, the sooner you can start taking actionable steps to move forward in the direction you want your life to take. You decide whether you will allow the hurt to make you a bitter or a better person. Learning from the hurtful situation gives you the confidence to emerge a much stronger and resilient individual.

Throughout our life's journey, we will all find ourselves plagued by unfortunate events and episodes that conjure up feelings of loss, insecurity, uncertainty, and fear. Unfortunate events are a fact of life and will happen to everyone. However, these experiences of adversity can often provide an opportunity to strengthen your character, deepen your emotional fortitude, and increase your overall sense of self and self-worth.

Failure is not an accident; it results from actions, inactions, and reactions to your environment or situation. So, if you encounter failure, stop blaming others for your limitations or failures and look to the one place where limitations and insecurities breed and can be transcended in your own mind. Do not give power to failure and trust your inner compass to map out the route to success.

Along the journey of your life, there will be challenges and tough times, but it is imperative that you choose to regard these as opportunities and not roadblocks. Even though you may not understand the why or the how, embrace the challenges you encounter and view them as learning opportunities. If nothing else, you can learn something from a challenging situation, something that you can use to help you at a later stage. Often, some of these challenges turn out to be blessings in disguise.

Deciding to learn something from a negative situation is the best strategy for coping with adversity. By simply asking what you can learn from a bad situation, you have changed your mindset. By changing your attitude, you stop focusing on being the victim and instead take control by choosing to make the adverse situation part of your informal education. The obstacle becomes the stepping-stone that will position you closer to your goals.

It will be extremely difficult for you to move forward with your life if you are fixated on a victim mentality. Unfortunate events are a fact of life and need to be separated from your personal self-worth. It is not what happens to you, but how you react to what happens to you that sets your life in motion. Your response to life's unfortunate events will determine how smooth or rocky your journey will be, and how many of those goals you can accomplish.

So, what may be perceived as unfair, a roadblock, or failure can really be a blessing in disguise. Maybe this option is closed to you because you are supposed to be doing something else or to keep you from harm. So, stop and look around you for another open door, and as you walk through that open door, you will understand impediment. The roadblock will disappear, and you can joyfully explore the new path destiny has paved for you.

Put all the negative experiences behind you, where they belonged, and where they should stay. You should not let this one experience define who you are as a person or your potential to move forward. Shift the power from the situation that is holding you hostage to viewing your life from an empowered position.

Once you can get off the road of self-pity and woe-is-me, change your attitude by simply asking what you could learn from this experience. Changing your attitude is a must, as it is not productive to harbor two powerful emotions at the same time. Each emotion will determine your mindset and next steps, and it is impossible to go in two different directions simultaneously. There is no way that you are going to move ahead while you are living with the bitterness and resentment of your past and allowing yourself to be an emotional hostage.

Sometimes, failure is the catalyst that provides the kick in the butt or the wake-up call many of us require and offers a fabulous learning opportunity. No one likes to be labeled a failure; however, sometimes we must hit rock bottom to learn some of the crucial lessons required to succeed.

So, have you really failed, or is life redirecting your efforts to a more meaningful experience? You need to stop long enough to reflect and capture the lessons that the experience has just delivered, so that you can turn it into success.

Failure has a definite purpose, structure, and sequence that ultimately leads you to greater heights in your life. So, take the time to understand your situation so that you can make a plan and take definite action to restructure your next move.

Do not allow yourself to be tainted by grief or guilt over what your life could have or should have been. Be confident that you are always in the right place at the right time, going through experiences that were necessary for your soul's development to grow in wisdom, endurance, and courage. So, stand proud of the person you are today and the one you will develop into tomorrow.

Every situation opens a door of opportunity if we stop long enough to assess the situation and walk through it. So, stop giving power to failure, and trust your inner compass to map out the route to a successful life.

Become an advocate for your skills, confidence, and strength, and not your insecurities and limitations. As a result, you will be more confident and poised and will soar, inspiring others as you overcome difficult times.

When you feel hateful and resentful, you are the one who suffers emotionally and physically. You wear yourself out and the other person may feel the same or may not even remember you or given you a second thought.

Be BETTER not BITTER, a powerful reminder to focus on personal growth and improvement rather than harboring resentment or bitterness. Your energy is better spent on positive transformation rather than dwelling on past grievances. Your response to life's challenges with either bitterness or a resolve to become better is completely up to you.

> *"You either get bitter, or you get better. It's that simple.*
> *You either take what has been dealt to you and allow it to make you*
> *a better person, or you allow it to tear you down. The choice does not*
> *belong to fate; it belongs to you."*
> **—Josh Shipp**

Find Someone or Something to Lean on

"You need someone to stand with you when it feels like everyone is standing against you."
—Paul C. Brunson

We all face times in our lives when the pain and the sorrow of a situation are just too much to bear; when we do not have the strength to move forward. During times of hopelessness, we must find someone or something to lean on for support. Turn to someone that will help you believe in your tomorrow. Someone who will support and guide you on your chosen path.

Coping with loneliness can be challenging, but there are several strategies you can try to ease the feeling. Here are some suggestions based on various expert sources:

1. **Partake in Group Activity:** Find a group that shares your interests and get involved as it can provide a sense of belonging and community. What are your interests? Reading, join a book club; physical fitness, join a gym. Is there something you've always wanted to learn more about? Enroll in a class where you'll meet like-minded people. Consider joining clubs, attending local events, or volunteering. And remember, you're not alone—there are many people out there who would love to connect with you. There is no excuse or justification for claiming loneliness as your constant companion.

2. **Give Your Time to Others:** Volunteering can help you meet new people and give you a rewarding sense of contributing to society.

3. **Take Time for Self-Care:** Treat yourself with compassion and self-care activities that make you feel good. Treat yourself to a movie, a special night out, a spa treatment, a relaxing massage, manicure/pedicure, whatever pampering means to you.

4. **Strengthen Face-to-Face Connections:** Attempt to create deeper connections with people by being fully present during interactions. It is easy to get engrossed in the virtual realm that today's digital world offers. Use your free time to nurture relationships rather than withdrawing into solitary activities. Be open to forming new friendships. It might be intimidating, but it can be very fulfilling. Cultivate meaningful connections with family, friends, and partners. Invest time in building strong relationships, practicing empathy, and maintaining open communication.

5. **Share Your Feelings with Others:** Talking about your feelings with someone you trust can help lessen the feeling of isolation. Soliciting feedback from your friends and family may help you validate those strengths and ultimately your passions in life. However, you must gauge the feedback with your internal source. Does the feedback resonate with you?

6. **Stop the Comparison Game:** Understand that life is different for everyone and avoid comparing your life to others. Everyone has their own path to walk.

7. **Engage with Audio Content:** Listening to music or podcasts that interest you can provide a sense of connection.

8. **Don't be a loner:** "A good friendship is a wonderful antidepressant," says psychologist Janice Kiecolt-Glaser, director of the Institute for Behavioral Medicine Research at the Ohio State University College of Medicine. Make time for friends and family. Connect and nurture old friendships. Reminisce about your time and life experiences and reawaken some of your younger days. Sometimes a simple text message can uplift your day. In this digital age, technology has revolutionized the way we connect with others. Whether it's through video calls, social media, or messaging apps, we can stay in touch with friends and family no matter where they are. Loneliness doesn't have to be a constant companion; there are so many ways to reach out. Remember, it's okay to feel lonely and reaching out for professional help is also a valid option if the loneliness persists.

Leaning on someone is not a sign of weakness, in fact, it is a sign of strength when you swallow your pride and admit that you need help.

Bottling up your pain and true feelings will not help you overcome the situation.

Once you have surpassed your situation, you can then be that someone that someone else can lean on. You can be that person who understands exactly what they are going through.

View your life from an empowered and positive vantage point. View those challenges that life sends to you as a necessary experience for the development and perfection of your soul.

It's important to connect with others, build relationships, and share experiences. Whether it's through social activities, hobbies, or simply reaching out to friends and family, human connection is essential for our well-being.

In those instances, when you have to find pleasure alone, discover activities you love doing by yourself and embrace the peace that comes with solitude. Being alone does not mean you have to be lonely.

> *"Life is not a solo act. It's a huge collaboration, and we all need to assemble around us the people who care about us and support us in times of strife."*
> **—Tim Gunn**

Embrace New Beginnings

"New beginnings are often disguised as painful endings."
— **Lao Tzu**

We must embrace new beginnings because whether or not we like it, the world is always changing, as nothing stays the same. Just like when we get married, divorced, a child is born, or a loved one dies, we know that our lives will change dramatically. These major turning points represent a point of no return. Your life will never be the same. These major changes occur when we have come to the end of the old and are on the cusp of a new chapter in our lives. Whether you embrace the change, resist it, or deny it, it is natural to feel apprehensive about what lies ahead.

Managing change means effectively managing our perceptions and fears. Change is the natural circle of life that brings about progress. Even though we can intellectualize that change is inevitable, we fight to keep the status quo, we try to hang on to what is most familiar. Clinging to the way things used to be may give a person a sense of security, but growth and progress can only come when we embrace change and accept the new opportunities and possibilities that come with new beginnings.

We all experience and manage change in different ways, with some reacting unpredictably and irrationally. If change is our idea, we embrace it enthusiastically, excited about the possibilities. However, if change is imposed upon us, we rebel and resist adapting to change. We need to embrace change as a normal part of our lives rather than a source of internal conflict, resistance against established norms, or contention with others. Our reaction, attitude, and perception of the change can either be an anchor that weighs us down or a catalyst that elevates us to greater achievements. If not managed correctly, the emotions associated with change can be difficult to navigate, as we often become our own worst enemy and unwittingly sabotage our progress with negative thoughts and beliefs.

When the change involves a perceived personal loss, the process becomes much more complex and harder to overcome as you go through periods of denial, anger, depression, and finally acceptance. You may move back and forth between a couple of cycles and back to the beginning, with each iteration lasting less time as you move more quickly through each cycle, until finally you wake up one day and it is just a fleeting thought.

Everyone perceives change differently. Some react positively, with renewed energy and excitement, while others have a more pessimistic view and perceive the change as the beginning of the end for them. As a result, they become stressed, overwhelmed, and sometimes bitter individuals.

Change does not have to be stressful, overwhelming, or confusing if you manage your perceptions and fears. The transition period from the old to the new is the time to figure out how you can maximize your new environment. This is the perfect time to revisit your life and clearly delineate what you want and envision for yourself. This may require that you leave behind some of the old ways that no longer resonate with you.

Change, whether planned or unplanned, imposed, or self-imposed, wanted or not, is necessary for your growth. Refrain from making assumptions, jumping to conclusions, and taking the change personally before you can weigh and assess all the facts.

Take it one day at a time and remember that it is your perception of change that affects your thoughts, feelings, actions, and reactions. Stop to examine how you perceive the change and determine whether you are helping or hurting yourself with your perceptions. Embrace new beginnings and let go of what is familiar and comfortable.

Stop rehashing where you came from and how things were; instead, get excited about where you want to go and how you are going to get there. Stop dragging your past and its remnants into your present. Hanging on to 'used to be' does nothing for your personal growth. What it does is keep you hostage to your past making it difficult to maintain optimism for your future and enjoying present moments. By continuously reaching back for your yesterday, you risk overlooking the joys and opportunities of today and the promise of tomorrow.

Have the courage to embrace the new opportunities, the new beginnings that come with change. Release the past and muster the energy to live with renewed purpose. If you perceive the change as an opportunity for a fresh start, a chance to change direction, you can travel through the transition highway with few or no problems at all.

It is okay to feel nervous, anxious, or sad to see your life moving in a different direction. However, you should not view this change as good or bad. Change simply signals the end of a cycle in your life and is a necessary event that will transition you to the next phase in your life.

It is beneficial to view change as necessary for your personal growth. Embrace change and align your words, thoughts, actions, and reactions with your goals, and do not let perceived obstacles distract you. Embrace the process of personal growth, let go of negativity, and surround yourself with individuals who bring positive contributions to your journey. Similar to a snake shedding its skin to uncover a fresh layer, shed the past and its remnants to reveal a stronger and more resilient version of yourself. Revel in the excitement of the endless possibilities and uncharted territories you will venture into, along with the exceptional chance to reinvent yourself.

It is essential to have patience with yourself as you transition from the old to the new. You have made monumental strides and gained a great deal of practical experience and wisdom. All this learning took time and effort and culminated in being the incredible person you are today. Capitalize on all that experience and put it to work for you in your new environment.

Just in case all else fails, fall back on the Serenity Prayer: *"God, grant me the serenity to accept the things I cannot change, the courage to change the things I can, and the wisdom to know the difference."*

Walking the walk of your chosen path

As we embark on our chosen journey, we often encounter twists, turns, and unexpected detours. Each step we take shapes our experience, and sometimes the most impactful moments happen when we least expect them. Each step becomes a decision, a commitment to the direction you've chosen.

Walking the walk of your chosen path, your soul's journey, is a personal endeavor. It's about reconnecting with your inner wisdom, releasing attachment to the ego, and manifesting your highest potential in this lifetime.

> *"Walk yours with integrity and wish all others peace on their journey. When your paths merge, rejoice for their presence in your life. When the paths are separated, return to the wholeness of yourself, give thanks for the footprints left on your soul, and embrace the time to journey on your own."*
> **- Unknown**

CHAPTER 4

EASING THE WALK OF YOUR CHOSEN PATH

Stress is an ignorant state. It believes everything is an emergency."
— **Natalie Goldberg**

Navigating life's difficulties involves understanding the inherent fluctuating nature of life, cultivating resilience, being flexible to go with the flow, practicing self-care, to name a few. Easing your days as you walk your chosen path is possible.

Some choose a difficult, stressful path to walk while others have an easier life. Being and staying optimistic during life's challenges can be easier said than done. However, there are steps you can take to help you navigate stressful, challenging events in your life. Any action taken to ease your walk can help you cope with the challenges you will encounter, as your individual chosen path is full of twists, turns, and unexpected events.

Coping with stress is essential for maintaining overall well-being. Some strategies that may help you manage stress and unexpected challenges in life are presented in the next few pages. Again, take what works for you and leave the rest behind.

Chronic Stress

Chronic stress is defined as a prolonged and constant feeling of stress caused by the everyday pressures of family and work or by traumatic situations and can have detrimental effects on your physical and mental health. Stress is an unavoidable part of life. How we respond to stress can help us learn and grow.

Stress affects nearly every system in the body, either directly or indirectly. Humans have a built-in mechanism to manage short- term acute stress but not chronic stress, which persists over an extended period. Your response to stress is shaped by various factors, including genetics. The genes that regulate the stress response help maintain a relatively stable emotional level, occasionally preparing the body for fight-or-flight reaction.

Fight-or-flight is the body's natural response to a perceived threat. In physiological terms, a tiny region in the brain called the hypothalamus sets off an alarm system in your body, which then prompts the adrenal glands (located atop the kidneys) to release hormones like adrenaline and cortisol. Adrenaline increases heart rate, blood pressure, and energy levels, while cortisol affects glucose levels, immune responses, and other bodily processes.

In chronic stress, the fight-or-flight reaction is constantly turned on which exposes the body to excessive cortisol, adrenaline, and other stress hormones that can negatively affect your entire body leading to many health problems such as heart disease, heart attacks, strokes, high blood pressure, sleep disorder, and many others. These symptoms can vary in their severity from one person to the next.

It isn't always easy to recognize chronic stress. When it is pervasive and long-lasting, people often grow so accustomed to the stress that it feels normal. To manage chronic stress, it is important to understand what it is, what may be causing it, and how it affects the entire body.

Chronic stress is a consistent feeling of being pressured and overwhelmed over an extended period. Individuals dealing with chronic stress might experience various symptoms, including:

- **Physical discomfort** such as muscle tension, headaches, or other types of body aches.
- Persistent sense of **fatigue** and a decrease in energy levels.
- **Sleep disturbances**, like insomnia or inconsistent sleep patterns.
- An impact on **mental clarity**, resulting in difficulty focusing or muddled thoughts.
- A sensation of being **trapped** or a perceived lack of control over their circumstances often describing a feeling of being "stuck."

It's important to note that not everyone will exhibit all these symptoms. However, if a person is experiencing three to five symptoms for several weeks, it could indicate they are suffering from chronic stress.

According to Harvard Health Publishing: "You can counteract the damaging effects of stress by calling upon your body's rich potential for self-healing." You can take simple steps that will help you minimize stress and lead a happier, healthier life, and create a learning journey that is fun, friendly, and most importantly, free of stress and anxiety.

Fortunately, you can harness your inner power to help you navigate stressful periods. There are several evidence-based strategies that can help you reduce stress and improve your overall mental health. Effective techniques for alleviating stress encompass a variety of activities such as ensuring adequate sleep, seeking more opportunities for laughter, listening to music, turning down extra work or commitments, pursuing financial independence, and choosing peace and happiness. These strategies are among the more common ones that many individuals find relatable. Yet, stress relief is highly personal, and what works can differ from one person to another. The point is to identify the activities that help you relief stress.

Make Sleeping a Priority

Sleep plays a crucial role in managing stress and is one of the most important things you can do to minimize stress. Consistently getting a full night's sleep can significantly lower stress and anxiety levels, and it's beneficial for overall health. The value of a good night's sleep or a simple nap cannot be underestimated. Sleep is self-care and a way for the body to rejuvenate itself.

Life is busy, but you can make it a point to improve your sleeping habits. For example, you can set a specific bedtime. Turn off the television, the electronics, and cell phone. Forgo the late-night movie or staying out late hanging out with friends. Stay home and schedule time to relax.

Research shows that the way you feel during the day, in part depends on how you slept the night before. Lack of sleep can affect your overall health, mood, how well you think, react, work, learn, and get along with others.

The benefits of a restful night's sleep on the brain are significant, affecting mental performance and health. The effects of quality sleep are tangible; it enables the brain to function optimally. During sleep, the brain prepares for the upcoming day by creating new connections that facilitate learning and memory. It enhances one's capacity for problem-solving and innovation. Sleep also plays a key role in regulating the brain's emotional center and areas that govern self-regulation, essential for emotional balance. Additionally, it supports brain health by clearing out harmful proteins that, if built up, can impair memory.

Insufficient sleep, on the other hand, can lead to health problems such as impaired cognitive performance, slower reaction times, and difficulties with learning and decision-making.

As adults, we recognize the importance of sleep for children's growth and development, often enforcing strict bedtimes to ensure they get the rest they need. Yet, it's common for adults to overlook the same principles for their own sleep habits. Establishing and adhering to a consistent sleep routine is just as crucial for adults, as it supports overall health, cognitive function, and well-being. It's beneficial for adults to apply similar boundaries to their sleep patterns to maintain a healthy lifestyle.

Sleep is much more than just a time for rest. It's an essential process for maintaining both brain health and overall functionality. During sleep, the brain engages in various critical activities that are vital for cognitive functions.

Good sleep is fundamental not only for feeling rested but also for the brain to perform its necessary functions effectively.

Laugh More

It is true that "laughter is the best medicine" as it is one of the best stress relievers. It is more than just a folk tale as it can benefit your overall health. Laughter can help reduce stress, boost your immune system, and many other health benefits. "Just a few minutes of laughter a day can improve your health in more ways than you might realize," explains Maria Heveran, a physician assistant at Geisinger's Lewisburg clinic. Laughing, whether a giggle, a belly laugh, or chuckle, feels not only good, but it is good for you and it is free. A bout of laughter can deliver powerful health benefits.

Why does it feel good to laugh? When you laugh, your body releases chemicals called endorphins. "Releasing endorphins can help increase the body's natural painkilling response," says Heveran. "This helps with chronic pain and can improve your mood."

These same endorphins help reduce stress. "Laughter is a valuable coping mechanism when we're feeling stressed," Heveran notes. "A hearty belly laugh can help start the day on a positive note and finish it on a relaxing one."

Laughing can reduce your body's production of stress hormones, thereby boosting your immune system. "It can also activate infection-fighting cells," says Heveran. "By managing stress with laughter, you'll help fight off stress reactions in the body."

Laughter naturally leads to deeper breathing, which enhances the circulation of blood to your organs. Moreover, deep breathing can anchor you in the present, reducing stress and anxiety both mentally and physically.

Every time you laugh, your lungs automatically breathe deeper thereby increasing the blood flow to your organs. This increased oxygenation of the lungs aids the heart in distributing oxygen-enriched blood throughout the body, promoting the growth of healthy cells. When cells are healthy, your organs function more effectively, contributing to an overall sense of well-being.

Laughter relieves stress and tension by relaxing your muscles. Watch a funny movie, standup comedian, and stay away from depressing news. Identify which activities you find to be funny and make it a point to engage in that activity at least once a week.

Listen to Music

Sing and dance like no one is watching or listening. Listening to music you love releases tension in the body. Music is one of the best remedies for stress and anxiety relief. In research by Suzanne Hanser, chair of the music therapy department at the Berklee College of Music in Boston, "making music can lower blood pressure, decrease heart rate, reduce stress, and lessen anxiety and depression."

Even the strongest person faces times when they aren't so strong and need help. Music helped me through one of the most difficult times of my life. Over the years, music has been a saving grace for me. Without it, I don't know how I would have made it through many of life's toughest challenges.

During my husband's illness, I wore a mask of false bravado trying to hide my true feelings of sadness. I did not have the luxury of breaking down, as I was his primary caregiver. But there were days when I felt an overwhelming sadness and found myself on the verge of breaking down unable to hold back my tears. During those moments, I'd step away from his side, get my earbuds, go to Apple music and search for my favorite salsa, merengue, or other dance music. I'd sing and dance until the overwhelming sadness subsided. Singing and dancing have always been passions of mine, and music has become a fundamental aspect of my existence. Whenever I am feeling sad, upset, overwhelmed, or even during happy days, I go to my music playlist where I can find the right song for the mood. Music has helped me through many challenging times by regulating my mood when nothing else works. Music has the power to soothe your mind, body, and soul. *"Music is to the soul what words are to the mind."* — *Modest Mouse*

Music provides a therapeutic feel for me and has always been a big part of my life. I'm certain it's the same for many others. My family can attest to the fact that I sing and dance and don't care if anyone is listening or watching.

My children and grandchildren have had to endure my singing since birth. I always sing to the children and the children love it. Every one of them had a special song. I'd wake them up with a good morning song and put them to sleep with a goodnight song.

When my kids were younger, I'd send them to my mother's house in the Dominican Republic for a few weeks during the summer vacation. One day I called to see how they were doing, and my older son asked to come home. I responded with the lyrics of the song *See You In September* (by The Happenings 1966). He was not happy with my response and said, "Do you have a song for everything?" I said "of course I do. There is a song for every occasion."

Research shows that music exerts a powerful influence on human beings. It can boost memory, build task endurance, lighten your mood, reduce anxiety and depression, stave off fatigue, improve your response to pain, and help you work out more effectively. Working with a music therapist is one effective way to take advantage of the many benefits music can have on your body, mind, and overall health.

Just Say "No"

Saying no doesn't mean you're selfish; it means you value your time. Politely decline commitments that don't align with your priorities. It's easy to say "yes" to a social invitation or take on extra work. However, many times we find ourselves overwhelmed when it comes time to deliver, as we find ourselves not only over committing but then we under deliver, which increases our stress levels.

Steve Jobs was the king of saying no. He said, "You have to pick carefully. I'm actually as proud of the things we haven't done as the things I have done. Innovation is saying no to 1,000 things." You cannot do it all. Saying "no" to activities, friends, or tasks that don't bring you joy frees up time for things that are a better use of your time. If you're feeling stressed out, practice turning down invitations that aren't improving your life and create space for the things you love.

Over committing one's time can lead to a delicate balancing act. When we stretch ourselves thin, we risk compromising the quality of our commitments. It's like trying to juggle too many balls at once—eventually, some will fall. To ensure that you do not over-commit, step back and think twice before taking on a new task. There will be times when you'll have to say no even to things you'd really like to do.

Besides saying no, you can avoid the perils of overcommitment by implementing a few strategies to manage your time.

- Prioritize your most important tasks and allocate time accordingly. Not everything deserves equal attention.
- Allow buffer time between commitments. Unexpected delays happen, and having some breathing room prevents stress. Give yourself some time to regenerate.
- Regularly evaluate your existing commitments. Are they still relevant? Can you delegate or renegotiate? Or can you just say 'no'?
- Quality over quantity–fewer well-executed commitments are better than many half-hearted ones.

Time is a precious commodity and a finite resource so allocating it wisely is crucial. Balance is the key.

Strive for Financial Freedom

Debt is often cited as one of life's greatest stressors, capable of significantly weighing you down. The dual burden of financial and psychological strain from debt can lead to ongoing emotional turmoil for you and your family. That stress eats away at the quality of your life and can leave you feeling powerless, angry, depressed, and helpless. It is extremely difficult to concentrate as your thoughts are engrossed with financial worries.

For instance, the solution of turning to your credit cards to help keep afloat during difficult financial times may seem like a necessary lifeline. However, it can also be extremely dangerous as your debts will continue to pile up and like a ship's anchor will drag you under. This creates a vicious cycle of "robbing Peter to pay Paul"—taking resources from one area to allocate to another, which is a short- sighted solution to the problem. Paying an overdue bill with your credit card solves your immediate problem quickly, but you'll have a credit card bill coming at you eventually.

The damaging effects of being in debt go far beyond the material and dig deep into the emotional and psychological health of human beings. Studies have shown that being in debt does indeed take its toll on the emotional and psychological aspects of our lives.

At its core is the element of fear: the fear of job loss and the subsequent loss of income, the anxiety over potentially losing valued possessions like a home or vehicle, and the overwhelming worry of falling into a financial pit too deep to escape. Such fears can lead to sleep disturbances and a diminished ability to concentrate. Stress becomes a constant companion, increasingly difficult to manage as time goes on.

Many people are at risk of falling into a state of depression when they end up losing their jobs and simply cannot afford anything at all. This only multiplies the feelings of anxiety and depression to where serious medical issues can arise. The entire family feels the anxiety, stress, and pain.

Being in debt is like being incarcerated, as it limits your options and narrows your range of choices. Being debt free gives you flexibility to do the things you want and not just limit yourself to those activities that are free. It frees up the cash that is devoted to monthly payments that you can now put towards savings, vacation, or educational pursuits. Knowing that you can keep your family afloat for three to six months in the event of a layoff or loss of income is priceless. Being debt free and having money in the bank gives you a sense of security that feels like a warm blanket on a cold winter night.

Striving for financial freedom is the goal. Financial freedom happens when you have enough cash and investments on hand to pursue the things you're enthusiastic about—regardless of how much they cost. By having financial freedom, you can make decisions that align with your values and life goals instead of worrying about how you'll make your next paycheck.

The Consumer Financial Protection Bureau states that these four components can better define financial freedom and well-being:

1. Having control over your day-to-day and month-to-month finances
2. Having the ability to absorb financial shock
3. Being on track to meet your financial goals
4. Making the choices that enable you to best enjoy life. Not having to live within the constraints of paycheck to paycheck

But where does one begin? Achieving financial independence and becoming debt-free involves a combination of strategies that focus on budgeting, saving, and reducing debt. Here are some key strategies:

- **Defining Financial Goals:** Determine what being financially free means to you and set precise financial targets with specific deadlines.
- **Develop a Budget:** Craft a monthly budget to oversee your spending and confirm that your savings are progressing as planned.
- **Automate Savings:** Establish an emergency fund and make automatic contributions to retirement accounts for steady growth of your savings. When you can, try to save one to two percent of your

earnings and, as your disposable income increases, increase your savings percentage.

- **Spending discipline:** Live within your means by spending less than what you earn and reducing superfluous expenses, which can help speed up debt repayment.
- **Strategies for Paying Off Debt:** To methodically tackle and clear your debts employ methods like the debt snowball— paying off debt from the lowest to the highest balance; or avalanche method—paying higher interest debt first.
- **Debt Reduction:** Focus on clearing high-interest debts like credit card balances and try not to roll over debt month-to- month.
- **Credit Score Vigilance:** Regularly monitor your credit score, as it plays a crucial role in your ability to secure loans with lower interest rates and favorable terms in the future.

These strategies are part of a broader approach to managing finances that can lead to a debt-free life and financial freedom. It's important to tailor these strategies to your personal financial situation and long-term objectives.

The journey to financial freedom is a marathon, not a sprint, and requires consistent effort and discipline. Be patient and as this is a short-term sacrifice for a long-term gain.

Choose Peace and Happiness

Choose peace instead of conflict. You do not have to partake in any situation where power struggles ensue. Rather than adding, a raised voice to a dispute, choose peace and happiness.

If conflict arises around you, you can opt for peace instead. Consider the adage "Choose your battles wisely" is a phrase that suggests one should be strategic and thoughtful about what issues to engage with. It means that not every conflict or problem deserves your time and energy, and sometimes it's better to focus on what's important. It's about recognizing that some issues may not be worth the effort, while others may require your full commitment.

It's a reminder to prioritize and to conserve your resources for the battles that really matter to you. It means that you can forgo fighting completely. When someone "pushes your buttons," they have simply invited you to take part in an interaction. Do not feel the need to accept this invitation. You can choose to disengage.

What makes you happy? How would you define true happiness? Is it getting your dream job, becoming independently wealthy, finding the love of your life, or having a baby? If you define happiness by obtaining things or relationships, then you are missing the one thing that can provide true long-lasting happiness.

True happiness comes from within. It comes from living your truth, being yourself, whatever that means to you. It means living an authentic life that frees you from the burden of trying to please others, including your own family.

Happiness is a state of being that you create. It's a choice that comes from within, no matter what's happening around you. Happiness is a magical emotion that has the power to dissolve crisis, heal illnesses, mend disagreements, and attract new opportunities.

You cannot fully control your environment, but you can control how you react. No matter what is going on around you, set your intention to stay lighthearted and loving in your outlook. Sometimes this may require that you step away from an unpleasant situation, go for a walk, workout, or do whatever makes you happy. Choosing happiness beats the alternative, which is being miserable.

True happiness is not feeling lonely when you are alone.

Easing the Walk of Your Chosen Path

Life's journey is a winding road, and every twist holds an experience necessary as a lesson for your soul's evolution. When fatigue weighs you down, stop to rest, take a time out to gather your thoughts and brace yourself for the rest of your journey. But here's the thing, you're not alone as others have walked this path before. These are people whose footprints are etched in time. These same people have left a legacy of courage, hope, and grace for you to lean on if you ask for help.

How people react to similar situations varies from one person to the other depending on their individual situation and life experience. You have the power to transform your reality by changing your mindset, attitude, and ultimately, your reality.

Go with the flow and allow yourself to be carried by the current of your dreams so it can lead you to your chosen path, where your dreams and destiny align.

"Happiness is a choice. You can choose to be happy. There's going to be stress in life, but it's your choice whether you let it affect you or not."
—Valerie Bertinelli

CHAPTER 5

PARENTING—TO BE OR NOT TO BE

"We have to prepare the child for the path, not the path for the child."
—**Tim Elmore**

The choice to have a child is a decision that is irreversible and will change your life forever. Deciding whether or not to have children is a tough decision because there is no way to get a test drive at parenting.

You may have many opinions about how to raise a child and what you would do in each situation. You can also have all the experience in the world of babysitting, but you will not come to fully understand the responsibility of parenting until after you have a child of your own. The parenting experience is akin to childbirth: you can watch videos, take Lamaze classes, get advice from others that have gone through the process, but until you deliver a child of your own, there is no way to fully grasp the magnitude of the experience.

In philosophical terms, we procreate because it is the 'circle of life.' Procreation represents birth, survival, and death. There is a continual equilibrium maintained by the births and deaths of people. My great granddaughter was born on the same day that one of my aunts died and ironically, about the same time.

Like many other things in life, having children is not for everyone. Notwithstanding, society expects us to procreate, so we do. In fact, people that make a conscious decision not to have children are frowned upon. I applaud women that who stand firm against societal expectations to bear children. No one should have children because of manipulation by a spouse, parent, or because it is what our society expects us to do. The decision should be made based on what the woman or couple knows to be in their best interest and not what others believe they should be doing with their lives.

I would argue that the choice to bring children into the world should require more thought, scrutiny, and justification than the decision not to have children. Prospective parents should consider that they will have to change their entire lifestyle to care for children that are vulnerable and will depend completely on them.

Are they willing to commit to an eighteen-to-twenty-one-year period of constant investment of capital, emotion, a guaranteed increased level of stress, loss of free time and peace of mind with no guarantee of a positive return on their investment?

One thing that expectant parents can count on getting is the longest roller coaster ride of emotions, from the sheer elation of your child's birth, first step, first word, graduation, wedding to all the grief and heartache they can inflict as teenagers.

Unfortunately, your child comes into this world without an instruction manual to help guide you in navigating the many challenges and protecting your investment.

Some parents seem to navigate the journey of parenthood with ease, from conception through to their child's university graduation and beyond, at least according to the image they portray. Others face the trials and tribulations of adolescence, the tumultuous teenage years, and other significant life challenges. Nevertheless, these are your flesh and blood, and you will do everything in your power to protect your children.

The fact is that some parents get a raw deal. Some silently wonder what happened to that wonderful child they once knew and loved. How did they produce a lemon from a beautiful apple orchard? Not only did this lemon fall from the tree, but it also grew in an apple orchard. Go Figure!

They may even wonder whether they brought the wrong child home from the hospital since there is no way this monster of a teen could be theirs. The child has none of the parents' attributes.

As your child grows from infant to toddler to pre-teen, you witness the many physical and psychological changes they go through. However, there is nothing that could prepare you for the transformation that occurs as they enter their teens. During their teens, your children are leaving the internal, sheltered, and protective environment that your family has cultivated, and they enter a phase of external focus. Many turn their backs on their immediate family and their values by partaking in risky behavior.

The Teenage Brain

Unlike that of an adult, the teenage brain hasn't matured enough for its different sections to work together effectively when assessing options, making decisions, and responding to various circumstances. As highlighted in an interview with Jay Giedd, M.D., there's a "second wave of development" that takes place. While the initial three years are critical, the subsequent sixteen years are equally significant. In the age span from 3 to 16, the brain undergoes considerable dynamic changes. The prefrontal cortex—often likened to the brain's command center—of the teenage brain is essentially a work-in-progress with many loose screws and wires and still in the process of development.

The prefrontal cortex is the section of the brain that weighs outcomes, forms judgments and controls impulses and emotions and communicates with the other sections of the brain through connections called synapses.

According to *The Parents with Teenagers Handbook,* by Damon Bachegalup "What scientists have found is that teenagers experience a wealth of growth in synapses during adolescence. During the teen years, the brain prunes away the synapses that it doesn't need to make the remaining ones much more efficient in communicating. In teenagers and into the mid-twenties, the brain develops in a back-to- front pattern. The frontal lobe, responsible for reasoning, planning, and impulse control, is one of the last areas to fully develop, sometimes not until around the age of twenty-five. So that the prefrontal cortex, that vital center of control, is the last fully develop.

Diagnostic image studies have shown that most of the mental energy that teenagers use in making decisions is in the back of the brain, whereas adults do most of their processing in the frontal lobe. An area of the teenager's brain that is well-developed early on is the nucleus accumbens, or the area of the brain that seeks pleasure and reward."

So, what does it mean to have an undeveloped prefrontal cortex with a strong desire for reward? "This combination could explain a lot of the stereotypical teenage behavior." This gradual development process is crucial for the complex integration of cognitive skills and emotional regulation that characterizes mature adult behavior. The tendency of teenagers to experiment with behaviors like sex, drugs, and alcohol could be attributed to the lack of connection between the brain's back and frontal regions.

Is parenting over-rated?

Do the stress, struggles, and challenges of raising children outweigh the joys? You rarely see both sides of the parenting coin. How often do you encounter someone telling you about their children's deficiencies from bad report card to disrespectful behavior? In fact, what you see is the opposite. You see parents covering up and making excuses for their children's faults. Maybe it is socially unacceptable for a parent to say that they have a lemon for a child.

The day-to-day life of most parents comprises doing endless chores from laundry to driving the kids around to and from activities and appointments and dealing with the financial impact of paying for braces, music lessons, and summer camp, and other extracurricular activity.

Several studies and scientific research have been conducted to gauge the impact of parenting on life.

In 2004, economist Daniel Kahneman conducted a research study with nine hundred working women in Texas. The study asked the women to rate their happiness associated with their day-to-day activities. Their findings revealed that taking care of children was overall a low point in terms of daily happiness. *Princeton psychology professor and Nobel laureate, Daniel Kahneman, and colleague and friend Amos Tversky were influential figures in the field of behavioral economics and decision-making.*

Additional research indicates that parents, compared to non-parents, encounter more pronounced emotional highs and more profound lows. These findings imply that the highs of parenting might offset the inherent challenges and difficulties. Dr. Arthur Stone noted that parents tend to experience more intense joys compared to those without children. Parents have more joy in their lives, but also, more stress and negative emotions as well.

A third study examined general trends in the link between parenting and life satisfaction, suggesting that parenting affects life satisfaction in distinct ways for different people at different points in their lives.

The study revealed that overall parents are happier than non-parents are. Moreover, this research also found that parents' happiness varies as a function of their child's age: People with children under age five and those with teenagers overall have less happiness than people with children ages 5 to 12, or older than seventeen. *(Research, conducted by Dr. Sonja Lyubomirsky at the University of California, Riverside).*

The decision not to have children is becoming more common in our society; however, these women feel the underlying pressure from friends and family to have children. After all, women have the responsibility to bear children, don't they? So, women who have transcended this pressure feel stigmatized by a society that has not moved on.

Some people may feel it's too expensive to have children. However, others would prefer to do something else with their time. Many women are torn between having a family and pursuing their careers. They must earnestly answer the question: Am I prepared to make the sacrifices required to break through the glass ceiling? More often than not, the answer is a resounding, "No, my family comes first." Some believe that choosing to pursue both motherhood and a career can sub-optimize both, leading them to opt for one or the other. Some of the most successful women in the corporate world have made a conscious decision not to have children, dedicating one hundred percent of their energy to their careers.

Choosing between work and family is a highly personal decision that takes many circumstances into consideration. Only you and your family can make the final decision. In the end, you have to be happy with your choice, whether you want to be a stay-at-home mom, a working mom, or childless and dedicated to your career.

According to the Pew Research Center, women that possess higher education are among the most likely to decide to be childless. These women are challenging our society's outdated paradigm that one must have children to live a happy and fulfilled life. According to the US Census data, one in five American women now end their childbearing years without having a child, compared with one in ten in the 1970s.

Parenting, at its core, is an integral part of your life's plan and purpose. There is no right or wrong choice when it comes to parenting; it is simply a part of your journey in this lifetime. Some women face medical issues that prevent them from having children. This is part of their path, to experience the feeling of not being able to bear fruit. Their mission may be to care for someone else's child through adoption or to lead a childless life.

Some opt to have children to satisfy the need for family, deep connection with others, bloodline continuity, the perception that it may bring happiness to a failing relationship; the reasons are endless. Having children is a very personal decision that may not require any specific thought process or justification.

Some pregnancies are planned and a matter of choice. Some are unplanned because of some unfortunate event or accident. In some cases, pregnancy can be a pleasant surprise after years of infertility. Most people do not take the time to analyze the choice to procreate. Even if they did analyze the choice to have children, their decision would be based on flawed assumptions because there is no way to fully understand the meaning of parenting until one has a child.

If you assume that some could fully analyze the decision, I will bet they would opt not to have children. Like waiting to have children until you can afford them, you'd probably never have a child.

While the choice to have children may be made for emotional reasons and impulses, it can also be made after careful consideration of all the information you have on hand. If you can choose, the decision should be given, at a minimum, the same time you give to any other major life event.

The minute your baby is born, you transition from the concept of being a parent to the reality of parenting. Regardless of how your child comes into this world, the transition is the same. You have taken the leap from being pregnant to being a parent.

The reality of the situation finally hits you. Your life will never be the same. You are now fully responsible for someone else's wellbeing. Not just anyone, your own flesh and blood and you are committed to being the best parent possible. This child depends completely on you for its survival. The responsibility of tending to the child's needs can be a source of energy, as this child has only you. You can't take a day off from being a parent, you cannot call in sick. You must be there for that child no matter what is going on in your life. This responsibility can also be a substantial source of stress.

Being and becoming a good parent means something different to everyone and one size does not fit all. Your knowledge or experience with children may not keep you from being overwhelmed by your own child. Even if you have experience with older children, each child is unique and will have his/her own challenges. You will need to take the time to know and understand the needs and wants of each child.

Even within the same family, three children raised identically can turn out completely different because each one has their own path to travel. For the most part, parents do the best they can for their children. The debate continues: is it nature or nurture that shapes them?

Parents have certain expectations for their children, and they rarely grow up to be how and what we want them to be. Part of being a parent is watching your kids grow, develop, and become independent. Many times, your children will make decisions with which you may not agree.

They try to protect their children from making some of the same mistakes they made, trying to save them from themselves. But guess what? Children must make their own mistakes. They must live the life they were born to live per their individual soul's journey, not their parents' expectations.

Many parents fool themselves into believing that they can control their children's destinies. However, the best they can do is give them a good foundation to fall back on, give them advice and support along the way. Then they must let go.

We must drop the "if my child fails, I've failed" attitude. Not true. You did the best you knew how, with the life experience, resources, and information you had.

Having children is like a "box of chocolates, you just never know what you are going to get" or what kind of parent you are going to be. Like everything in life, there will be good times and bad times but overall, it should be a rewarding experience.

If you are lucky, at about age 25, the required capital investments diminish, your teens become human, and suddenly, you become smarter in their eyes and hopefully a friend for life.

If you are extremely lucky, you get grandchildren, as they are your "gift from God for not killing your children."

"Parents can only give good advice or put them on the right paths, but the final forming of a person's character lies in their own hands."
— **Anne Frank**

CHAPTER 6

WHAT ABOUT RELIGION?

Religion is one of the most polarizing and sensitive issues to discuss. Although religions encourage peace and tolerance, few can remain calm and tolerant when defending their religious beliefs. Religion is very personal and controversial. More atrocities have been committed in the name of religion than any other cause.

When analyzing religion through the historical lens, we note that people have killed more individuals in the name of religion than in any other type of war. Throughout history, there have been many religious conflicts that have persisted for extended periods of time, resulting in the loss of thousands of lives. There are also countless examples of those who have murdered their spouses because divorce is against their religion. But murder isn't?

So, what is religion and why all the controversy?

There are many definitions for the term "religion" in common usage, ranging from the specific definition attributed by different sects to the broadest definition to include most, if not all belief systems. "Religion is any specific system of belief about deity, often involving rituals, a code of ethics, and a philosophy of life." *(ReligiousTolerance.org)*

With approximately twenty-one major world religions today, each claiming to be 'The One' true faith, no single religion commands a majority of the global population. There are also about twenty-three smaller religions with a well-defined belief in deity, humanity and the rest of the universe which have historical significance. There are also hundreds of faith groups in the world." *(Religioustolerance.org)*

"If we were to examine the basic principles of the religions of the world, we would find a great similarity. Each point to one central Life, from Whose Self-Existence, all draw their livingness, and without which nothing could exist. The Christian Religion gives more value to the individual life than do most of the others. In many respects, the Christian Bible is the greatest book ever written, and does truly point a way to eternal values. But it is only ONE explanation and cannot be considered the ONLY light on religion, for there are many others whose combined teachings weave the story of TRUTH into a complete and unified pattern." *(Science of the Mind, Ernst Holms)*

"There are approximately one billion people that do not profess belief in any religion." Do you blame them? Which group is 'The One'? Most thinking people are looking for something to believe in, but they also want to know the 'why' of such a belief, and how it works without all the mystery.

One size does not fit all. You must follow your heart and stick to what works for you and your personal growth and development without condemning someone else's belief system.

Since childhood, I've had trouble accepting the conventional religious dogma, questioning the nuns at my Catholic School and my mother on religious topics. Of course, the answers I received discouraged me from asking questions. It was the way it was, and one had to accept them, no questions asked. Still, in my mind, I had a difficult time processing the information. My gut feeling and intuition told me there must be another explanation.

I believed in the nonconventional philosophies that traditional religious groups condemned. I would seek bits of information from various sources, but it always fell short.

I pondered why I had never felt the overwhelming need to go to church or seek the association of any religious institution. I had gone to church and attended mass because my mother and our Catholic School would make us go. I stopped attending mass when I found myself just going through the motions, not really present. I had been there in body, but not in spirit, which led me to question the motives of those around me. Were they there because they were expected to or because they had a real calling?

Some people have used religion as an excuse to put others down, or draw a line in the sand, or to compete and kill. Religious snobbery is an extremely unattractive behavior, but very real. To me, this is another form of discrimination that turns people, like me, away from religion. Religious snobs can often be found in every belief system, looking down upon, criticizing, and condemning the people outside of their belief system. These people are not being compassionate; they are just being judgmental and snobbish with their holier than thou attitude.

During a conversation with a friend, I relayed my elation that my youngest son started taking Bible study lessons with the Mormons. It was great because it showed his willingness to change his way of life and that the Mormons would assist him in leading a better life. And in the end, "all religions lead to the same place." About an hour after this conversation, she called me back to tell me she felt compelled to tell me I was wrong, that all religions did not lead to God and salvation; and although I was a good person selflessly helping friends and family members, all of my good deeds, no matter how well-intentioned, would not save me; because the only way to get to God is through Jesús Christ. I responded by saying that this belief system is just one among many, and we all have the right to our own views and convictions. In matters of faith, we must stick with whatever works for us on a personal level.

I must admit that I was quite disturbed for days by this condemnation of my soul. According to her belief and interpretation of religion, only an approximate 4% of the entire population on earth will be saved and go to Heaven; and the other 96% of the population has gotten it all wrong.

From my personal point of view, some need religion as a crutch to help them stay on the right track. Some turn to religion to reassure themselves that it will lead to acceptance and forgiveness in the afterlife. They turn to religion and faith as solace for the soul. Some need the pre-digested philosophy, morality, and instructions for their daily lives, not having to think for themselves. Some aimlessly want to be told how to live their lives. Religion gives them the firm foundation upon which they can build their daily lives; it stops them from making costly mistakes and helps them find ways to care for others. In some cases, such as in people who need boundaries and rules, this framework is of vital importance.

While every religion has unique rituals and dogma, all seek to connect us with our spiritual source. They all honor the reality and presence of God and the importance of love, compassion, and kindness and the eternalness of life. These basic truths far outshine the individual ways religions express them. We can honor our differences while celebrating our unity, and then we can meet on common ground.

Spirituality versus Organized Religion

The comparison between spirituality and religion is a topic of deep contemplation and personal interpretation. Spirituality is often seen as an individual's personal journey towards understanding life's deeper meaning, a quest for connection with the universe, or a search for inner peace. It is a path that transcends the boundaries of formal religious practices and doctrines, focusing on the personal, inner experience. Spirituality is an innate, personal experience that transcends the structures and doctrines of organized religion.

Religion, on the other hand, typically involves organized beliefs and worship, often centered on a deity or deities, sacred texts, and rituals. It is a communal experience that can provide a sense of belonging, moral guidance, and a structured approach to spirituality. Both paths seek to answer life's big questions and provide comfort and meaning, but they do so in different ways. While religion offers a collective way to express spirituality, spirituality itself can exist both within and outside the framework of organized religion. Some find solace in the structure and community religion provides, while others prefer the freedom and individuality of a more personal spiritual practice. Ultimately, the choice between spirituality and religion is deeply personal and varies from individual to individual.

"Spirituality does not come from religion. It comes from our soul."
— **Anthony Douglas Williams**

CHAPTER 7

THE END OF YOUR CHOSEN PATH

> *"End? No, the journey doesn't end here.
> Death is just another path. One that we all must take."*
> **- J.R.R. Tolkien, The Return of the King**

Impermanence is an inherent aspect of our existence. Just as seasons change and stars burn out, all things eventually end. It's a poignant reminder to appreciate the fleeting moments in our lives. Death is the end of your chosen path, the end of your journey in this lifetime. Death is an extension of life. We are all eventually going to die.

Nothing lasts forever as there is no such thing as eternity on earth and everything must end. We all have that expiration date and time stamped on our souls. "There is no such thing as a premature or unplanned death, and unpleasantries associated with death are largely of the human imagination." Your soul's calendar plans the time, and death cannot occur one moment before that time is reached.

But here's the thing: death is not the end; it is the beginning of a new life in another dimension. Death, the ultimate and inevitable end of our mortal journey, is a profound and mysterious concept that transcends cultural boundaries and beliefs. Different philosophical, religious, and scientific traditions have varying perspectives on death.

Fear of Death

Fear of death is a complex and universal emotion that can manifest in various ways. We keep trying to make sense of death because we're afraid of it. Many people don't even like to talk about death. They live their lives as if they were going to live forever. If you bring it up, they think it is too morbid. How can they not be afraid to die since life is all they know?

It's always scary to step into change, and the more unknown that change is, the more daunting and unpredictable it feels.

Many fear death because for humans it represents the ultimate unknown. We don't know for sure what happens after we die, and this uncertainty can be unsettling. The fear of non-existence or the idea of facing eternal nothingness without friends and family can be distressing. In addition, many worry about their friends and families and leaving them behind.

One of the biggest fears of death is the potential physical pain and suffering. For some, the dying process itself can be painful and uncomfortable. Fear of pain, suffering, and the unknown aspects of the dying process contribute to the fear of death.

Another source of the fear of death are cultural and religious beliefs, which instill the fear of death. While some religious beliefs offer comfort by promising an afterlife, others may instill fear of judgment or punishment.

In its absence, we would possess indomitability. This absence of fear is the ultimate strength; it renders one impervious to harm.

Fear of death is a natural part of being human. Acknowledging this fear can lead to personal growth and a deeper appreciation for life. It is important to lose the fear of death, as it signifies a birth on another plane. Without the fear of death, we would be invincible. You can kill me, but you will not break my spirit. Freedom from this fear is the greatest power that exists, and it makes you invulnerable.

Change what you think is wrong with you or your life and take control of your life. Throw away your fear. In the end, the worst thing that could happen to you is death, and that just means the end of a game and the beginning of another one.

Transformative Voyage for a New Beginning

Many people view death as a new beginning, a transition from the physical world to a spiritual one. Many believe that death symbolizes the continuation of existence, with the soul embarking on a new journey beyond earthly boundaries. While death may mark the end of one's current life, it is not the final chapter, but the start of a fresh chapter in a different realm.

Death is often seen as a transformative voyage, where the soul liberates itself from the constraints of the physical body and enters a realm of heightened consciousness. This new state of existence is frequently depicted as a spiritual journey, where the soul evolves and gains profound wisdom that aids in its growth and enlightenment.

The concept of an afterlife or a different realm after death is a new form of existence that offers opportunities for spiritual development, self-reflection, and the exploration of deeper truths. Depending on individual beliefs and traditions, people may refer to this realm as heaven, paradise, nirvana, or other similar names.

The idea of experiencing a new life in a different realm after death suggests that we should not fear death but embrace it as a natural part of the cycle of life. It is a transition that allows the soul to let go of its earthly attachments and embark on a new spiritual journey. This perspective motivates individuals to live their present lives with purpose and mindfulness, knowing that death is not the end, but a continuation of their existence in a transformed state.

Death is indeed a profound and mysterious aspect of our existence on earth. It marks the culmination of our physical journey and often prompts contemplation about life, consciousness, and what lies beyond. While interpretations of death vary across cultures, religions, and philosophical traditions, from a biological standpoint, death occurs when the body's vital functions cease. Cells stop dividing, organs fail, and the intricate balance that sustains life unravels.

The cycle of life and death is fundamental to the natural world. Organisms are born, grow, reproduce, and eventually die, making way for new life. From a spiritual and philosophical viewpoint, death is a transition rather than an end. Some believe in reincarnation, where the soul continues its journey by inhabiting new bodies across lifetimes.

Various religious traditions posit an afterlife—such as heaven, hell, or other realms—where the soul faces judgment based on its deeds. Certain philosophies propose that the soul is eternal and transcends physical existence. Death merely frees it from the constraints of the body. In Hinduism and Buddhism, the Cycle of Samsara involves birth, death, and rebirth until one attains enlightenment (Nirvana).

"What the caterpillar calls the end, the rest of the world calls a butterfly" is attributed to the Chinese Philosopher Lao Tzu, though its exact origins are unclear. This quote speaks to the idea of transformation and perspective. Just like the caterpillar undergoes a metamorphosis to become a butterfly, what may seem like an ending can actually be the beginning of something new and beautiful. It's a reminder that change is a natural and essential part of life, and that new beginnings are often disguised as challenging or even painful endings.

Departure of the Soul

The transition from this earthly existence to the afterlife is a topic that has fascinated humanity for centuries. While beliefs and interpretations vary across cultures, religions, and spiritual traditions, there are some common themes and perspectives:

1. **Transition Beyond Life**
- Death is often seen not as a conclusion, but as a transformation from the material world to a spiritual existence.
- The soul's release from the physical body is sometimes depicted as a freeing moment, where the soul departs its corporeal confines.

2. **Journey of the Soul**
- Some belief systems describe the soul embarking on a journey after death. This journey may involve crossing a river, climbing a mountain, or passing through gates.
- In ancient Egyptian mythology, the soul faced judgment before Osiris, the god of the afterlife. The weighing of the heart determined the soul's fate.

3. **Near-Death Experiences (NDEs)**
- Some individuals who have experienced clinical death and been revived report NDEs. These experiences often involve feelings of peace, light, and encounters with deceased loved ones.
- While NDEs are subjective, they contribute to the belief that consciousness continues beyond physical death.

4. **Reincarnation**
- In Hinduism, Buddhism, and other Eastern traditions, reincarnation is central. The soul (Atman) is believed to take on new bodies in successive lifetimes.
- Reincarnation offers the opportunity for spiritual growth and learning.

5. **Heaven, Hell, and Purgatory**
   - In the teachings of Christianity, Islam, and Judaism, the afterlife is depicted as having distinct domains:
   - Heaven: An eternal sanctuary of joy and divine presence.
   - Hell: A place of retribution or estrangement from the divine.
   - Purgatory: An interim state where souls are cleansed prior to their ascent to heaven.
6. **Scientific and Philosophical Perspectives**
   - Scientifically, death is the end of all biological activity. Consciousness remains a mystery.
   - Philosophers are divided on whether our identity endures beyond death. Some advocate for materialism (consciousness is brain-dependent), while others support dualism (mind and body are distinct).
7. **Cultural Customs, Rituals, and Ceremonies**
   - Funeral rites, memorial services, and rituals vary widely. They serve as ways to honor the departed and provide comfort to the living.
   - Practices like lighting candles, reciting prayers, and performing specific rituals are believed to guide the soul's journey.

These are only a few of the many ways in which people have attempted to comprehend and articulate and describe the profound journey of the soul from this life to the next. Recall that these viewpoints are diverse, and different philosophies provide solace to different people. In the end, the mystery of the soul's departure remains a profound aspect of the human experience.

Deathbed Companions

How and when we bid farewell to this world is part of our chosen path and others should respect and honor our choice. Whether we yearn for a peaceful sunset, a serene room, or the dramatic embrace of nature, our last goodbye reflects our innermost desires and beliefs. As we approach the end of our earthly journey, we should find solace in knowing that our chosen departure will be a testament to the lives we have lived and the love we have shared.

The individuals we choose to have by our side during our last moments reflect our deepest desires and beliefs. Whether it be family, friends, or spiritual mentors, each presence brings forth a distinct energy that can provide comfort, support, and a sense of peace as we transition from this life to whatever lies beyond. Some people find comfort in the familiar faces of people they have lived with their whole lives, while others seek tranquility in seclusion, longing to bond with the infinite cosmos.

The presence of family members at a dying person's bedside is often driven by the family's own needs and fears rather than the needs of the dying individual. Some people may choose to die alone, waiting for a moment when no one is present, to protect their loved ones from the pain of witnessing their final moments.

Some people regret leaving a loved one's deathbed, only to have the person pass away shortly after. This phenomenon can be understood in two ways:

Subconscious Coping Mechanism: Those who step away might subconsciously recognize their emotional limits and choose to leave, knowing they can't handle the situation. The emotional weight of witnessing a loved one's final moments can be overwhelming, and stepping away can be a way to protect oneself.

Dying Person's Preferences: The dying individual might have specific reasons for wanting certain people around. Confronting death can lead to significant personal growth and a deeper understanding of life and spirituality. This process is deeply personal and varies from person to person. As such, some people may opt to be alone during their passing or only want specific people around

The diagnosis was stage four breast cancer with a 20% survival, and I cried. As my friend consoled me, she assured me that everything was going to be okay. But this was my friend, the nurturer. Even in the face of the most devastating news a woman could get, she felt compelled to console her friends. As we hugged and consoled each other, all the tension and ill feelings of the last couple of years melted away. I knew I had to be there for my friend in her time of need.

Helplessness is the only word I can think of to describe how I felt during her illness. She was going through so much with the surgeries and the chemotherapy, and there was absolutely nothing I could do to help ease her pain.

I remember thinking how I wished I could help her with his burden by taking on some of her pain. I wished I could take a couple of her chemo and radiation treatments to ease her ordeal, but I could not. This was her path to walk; there was nothing I could do to lessen her struggle. All I could offer was my support and presence. To sit by her side as she rested or to pamper her with a pedicure—small comforts in her time of need.

Our friendship spanned 16 years, with the last two being tumultuous the reasons for which were unclear to me. Looking back, it seems as if fate was bracing me for her eventual passing. She was one of the few people in my life I called a friend. In fact, she was more like a sister to me. Whenever I had news, good or bad, she was the first person I called. We shared many wonderful years of friendship.

Our lives, personalities, likes, and dislikes were completely different. Our lifestyles were at different ends of the social spectrum during the first 15 years of our friendship. I was married with children. She was single and childless. She had a wide circle of friends, while I could count my friends with one hand and have fingers left to count. When she was out traveling or out on a Friday or Saturday night, I was home tending to my family. Yet, despite our differing paths, we shared a bond over our New York roots and our workplace—a connection that bridged our disparate worlds.

The week she passed away I had gotten news that her closest friends were traveling to Virginia to visit. I thought this was a routine visit and decided that I would not invade their privacy. After all, I lived in Virginia and could stop by anytime. The weekend they came into town, I spent one day catching up with the girls then stayed away.

That Wednesday, while I was at work, I got the news that she had passed away. Although I knew she was dying, the news felt like a punch in the gut. I did not know that her doctors had given her two weeks to live, and her friends had come into town to see her off. No one thought to let me know.

The night she passed away, she had requested that her friends sleep in her bedroom, a last sleepover. She died surrounded by her best friends and her mother.

Nothing hurts more than discovering that you have allowed yourself to be duped into believing in a relationship that never really existed. The day you receive the wake-up call you see that everything you thought and believed was a lie. Suddenly, you see the wall that sheltered you from truth come crumbling down. *"To the heart and mind, ignorance is kind. There's no comfort in the truth. Pain is all you'll find."*

Can you imagine continuing to stay friends with someone who continuously shuns you? How pathetic is that? This relationship with my so-called best friend was a lie that lasted for about 20 years. While I was referring to her as my best friend, she only considered me a mere acquaintance. How could that be? How can two people view a relationship in such a diverse way?

I was an unconditional friend that would have supported her in anything she did. However, there were many signs and evidence that she really did not feel the same way about our friendship. I always suspected that she was not a genuine friend, but to me she was like a sister, someone I could talk to about anything. I wish she had been more honest about how she felt. In hindsight, she did, in her passive-aggressive way, try to let me know; I was just ignoring all the cues. Not only was I not part of her inner circle of friends, but frequently, she completely stopped talking to me for no apparent reason.

When I was getting divorced, I turned to her for support during one of the most difficult times in my life. I asked her to accompany me to lawyers office to witness the execution of my divorce documents. The reaction I got from her was completely unexpected. It was judgmental and non-supportive. For me, this was the last straw. That is when I knew I had to walk away from this so-called toxic friendship.

The last time she stopped talking to me, I decided I was going to stop dealing with her immature emotional outbursts altogether, regardless of the years of friendship. I was so fed up with her I struggled with attending her wedding. I felt she had invited me simply out of sheer obligation and the number of years that we had known each other and the fact that I lived a mere five miles from her home. She did not really want me there, and I did not want to attend. But we both did the 'right' thing merely because of the optics of not inviting me and me not attending.

A few months after her wedding, she received the diagnosis of breast cancer. There was no way I could turn my back on her. I continued to visit and support her during her illness. She battled this disease for five long years and then passed away. At least I was a genuine friend to her, even though she really did not reciprocate the friendship.

Sorting through her pictures to prepare a collage for the viewing confirmed all of my suspicions about the strength of our friendship. This exercise was an eye opening experience for me. Her pictures and memorabilia told of a life surrounded by friends and family. Out of the hundreds of pictures we viewed, I found myself included in one, maybe two. It was painfully clear to me who her real friends were, and I was not one of them.

The one picture that sealed it for me captured the moment at her wedding. There she was in her wedding dress, surrounded by her four closest friends. These were the same ladies that were by her side when she died. She even shunned me at the very end. But this was her choice to make, and I had to respect and honor her decision. It's been said that people decide whom they want around at the time of their death. You repeatedly hear people tell stories of how they were with their loved ones every minute of the day for weeks, and when they decide to walk away for a moment, the person dies. This leaves the grieving person kicking themselves for having walked away. The truth may be that the person was waiting for them to walk away in order to pass away. For whatever reason, they did not want that specific person around.

So, I honestly believe that my friend had chosen the people she wanted around. These were the same ladies she had shared decades of memories and wonderful experiences with, so it was only right that they saw her off to the other side.

Your Legacy and Beyond

Beyond our physical departure, we leave behind a legacy—a ripple in the cosmic pond. Our deeds, memories, and the impact we've had on others continue to resonate. The love inside, you take it with you and that love leaves an indelible mark on those left behind. Whether it's a whispered story, a cherished photograph, or a lesson learned, our essence lingers in the hearts and minds of those who remain.

Reflecting on our presence and the path of our spirits, the connection between life and death becomes intricately interwoven. The transition from life to death is a profound and mysterious journey that has captivated human minds for centuries. While individuals may hold diverse beliefs and viewpoints on this subject, there is a shared intrigue with the shift from existence to the unknown.

Tapestry of Life and Death

In the expansive tapestry of existence, the interconnected strands of life and death influence each other deeply, with both playing a significant role in shaping the other. Our relentless curiosity propels us towards exploring the enigmas that exist beyond the boundaries of the known.

The concept of death is the beginning of a new life in a different realm, symbolizing the completion of a person's spiritual journey in their current existence. It is a transformative process that allows the soul to continue growing and evolving beyond the physical world. This perspective offers solace and hope, emphasizing the belief in an existence after death or a fresh start after death.

In the grand tapestry of life and our fleeting existence, death remains an enigma—a threshold we all will eventually cross. Whether it signifies an end or a continuation, it compels us to contemplate our beliefs, cherish our memories, and seek meaning in our life.

So, as we walk our soul's path, let us honor both life and death— the intertwined threads that shape our existence.

YOUR POWER WITHIN – INNER GUIDANCE

Your inner strength and guidance can lead you through life's challenges and empower you to overcome obstacles. Together, your inner strength and guidance are like a compass and an anchor; they help you navigate through the storms of life and keep you grounded in your true self. They empower you to overcome obstacles by providing clarity, motivation, and the courage to persevere. The answers you seek often lie within you, and by tuning into your inner wisdom, you can find the direction and strength needed for the journey of your soul.

Thank you for joining me on this writing journey. May the insights and reflections found within these pages continue to resonate within your heart and soul. May your path be illuminated with wisdom and may the light of self-discovery guide your steps.

With a heart full of gratitude for our shared journey into the depths of the spirit, Namaste.

> *"The balance and peace we seek for ourselves, and our society won't be achieved through mental effort alone. Mind and spirit are meant to travel together, with spirit leading the way. Until we make a conscious commitment to understand and embrace our spiritual nature, we will endure the ache of living without the awareness and guidance of the most essential part of ourselves."*
> **—Susan L. Taylor**

YOUR NAME

Author: Edgar Albert Guest (1881 - 1959)

You got it from your father. It was all he had to give.

So, it is yours to use and cherish, for as long as you may live. If you lose the watch he gave you, it can always be replaced.

But a black mark on your name can never be erased.

It was clean the day you took it and a worthy name to bear, when he got it from his father, there was no dishonor there. So, make sure you guard it wisely, after all is said and done, You'll be glad the name is spotless when you give it to our son.

ABOUT THE AUTHOR

Blanca De La Rosa was born in the Dominican Republic. She grew up in the projects of the upper west side of Manhattan in New York, during the time before the Hispanic population developed the supportive Latino community that exists today. Although she struggled without support in her cultural and linguistic transition, De La Rosa graduated from Pace University with a bachelor's degree in international business management and to establish a successful thirty-four-year career rising through the ranks of Mobil Oil then ExxonMobil Oil Corporation.

During her career, she held numerous positions, both domestic and international, in nature with increasing responsibility. These assignments took her around the United States, Europe, Central and South

America, and Nigeria. De La Rosa retired from ExxonMobil after thirty-four years of service.

As a business development manager and president of the company's employee resource group, she represented her company as lead presenter at the Regional and National Scholarship Awards hosted by the Hispanic Heritage Foundation. Also, she represented her company as host, keynote speaker, and panelist of various events with organizations supported by the company's charity foundation. After thirty-four years in the industry, she says her most rewarding role was serving as a mentor to the younger employees in her company—guiding them through the corporate maze.

OTHER WORKS BY BLANCA DE LA ROSA

What would you give up today for a better tomorrow? Many individuals give up the only world they know in pursuit of a better tomorrow. Four inter- connected stories spanning over 100 years is an inspiring cross-generational journey from Spain to the US. focusing on one of the main characters in a given era. Their personal stories illustrate the challenges and opportunities of immigration, acculturation, coming of age, and self-discovery through the characters' psychological and moral growth. De La Rosa shares her coming- of-age story of self-discovery as she transitioned from New York City's pro- jects to corporate America, detailing her personal and professional journey.

¿A qué renunciarías hoy por un mañana mejor? Muchas personas renuncian al único mundo que conocen en busca de un mañana mejor.

A lo largo de más de cien años, En busca de un mañana mejor no es sólo una memoria que retrata la historia de tres generaciones, sino más bien un viaje intergeneracional desde España hasta Estados Unidos.

La novela transporta al lector a una época largamente olvidada con una descripción histórica legible de los taínos, los conquistadores, los primeros colonos, el Imperio español y la República Dominicana, intercalados en la narrativa a través de la perspectiva del personaje de la época.

BLANCA DE LA ROSA

Insider's guide for coping with the challenges in the corporate maze with uplifting and inspiring advice.

Discover how to assess the journey of your career, manage a bad manager, deal with career failure, and develop a career road map.

Offers a fresh approach and insight on climbing the corporate ladder to in- crease the chances of success in the workplace.

Taking a holistic approach can apply to your career, as upward mobility in any organization requires much more than a degree. Getting ahead requires that you are well-rounded. Understand and abide by those unwritten and unspoken rules

Develop a career plan—develop a forward-looking perspective. Take charge of your career by having a clear direction of your goals and aspirations

Strategic Planning Discover how it can help you succeed in career and prosper in your personal endeavors.

Translation of the novel El color de agosto by Lis Meler

Elena thrived as a businesswoman in a male-dominated industry,. However, an unexpected event during a business trip abruptly ends her career as mana- gement confronts her and dismisses her.

Following the dismissal, Elena seeks solace in the house, where she spent her summer days as a youth reconnecting with her past. A past that had always been at the forefront of her mind now seems to pave the way for her future.

BIBLIOGRAPHY

1. "Lotus Flower Symbolism," Lotus Flower Meaning, accessed April 19, 2019, www.lotusflowermeaning.net/symbolism.php
2. "Good instincts usually tell you what to do long before your head has figured it out." ~ Michael Burke, https://www.quotes.net/quote/38642
3. http://balagan.info/timeline-for-the-second-rif-war-1909.
4. Browne, Sylvia. Adventures of a Psychic: The Fascinating and Inspiring True- Life Story of One of America's Most Successful Clairvoyants (1990)
5. Browne, Sylvia. "Life on the Other Side: A Psychic's Tour of the Afterlife" (1999)
6. Browne, Sylvia. "Angels and Spirit Guides: How to Call Upon Your Angels and Spirit Guide for Help" (1999)
7. Browne, Sylvia. "The Other Side and Back: A Psychic's Guide to Our World and Beyond" (1999)
8. Browne, Sylvia. "The Other Side of Life: A Discussion on Death, Dying, and the Graduation of the Soul" (2000)
9. Browne, Sylvia. "Soul's Perfection" (2000)
10. Browne, Sylvia. "Blessings from the Other Side: Wisdom and Comfort from the Afterlife for this Life (2000)
11. Browne, Sylvia. "The Nature of Good and Evil" (2000)
12. Browne, Sylvia. "Past Lives, Future Healing: A Psychic Reveals the Secrets to Good Health and Great Relationships" (2001)

13. Browne, Sylvia. "Prayers" (2002)
14. Virtue, Doreen. The Lightworker's Way: Awakening Your Spiritual Power to Know and Heal. Hay House, 1997
15. Virtue, Doreen. Archangels and Ascended Masters: A Guide to Working and Healing with Divinities and Deities. Hay House, 2003.
16. Virtue, Doreen. Healing With the Angels: How the Angels Can Assist You in Every Area of Your Life (1998)
17. Virtue, Doreen. Archangels and Ascended Masters: A Guide to Working and Healing with Divinities and Deities (2003)
18. Virtue, Doreen. Angel Numbers: The Angels Explain The Meaning Of 111, 444 And Other Numbers In Your Life (2005) - An exploration of angelic numerology.
19. Virtue, Doreen. Messages from Your Angels: What Your Angels Want You to Know (2002)
20. Https://annasayce.com/your-soul-chose-one-of-these-4-reasons-to-incarnate/

www.ingramcontent.com/pod-product-compliance
Lightning Source LLC
Chambersburg PA
CBHW030039100526
44590CB00011B/269